Silent
Killers
of
FAITH

DR. STEPHEN CROSBY

Silent Killers of FAITH

Overcoming Legalism and Performance-Based Religion

Treasure House

An Imprint of

Destiny Image® Publishers, Inc.

P.O. Box 310
Shippensburg, PA 17257-0310

"For where your treasure is, there will your heart be also."
Matthew 6:21

ISBN 0-7684-2957-9

For Worldwide Distribution
Printed in the U.S.A.

This book and all other Destiny Image, Revival Press, MercyPlace,
Fresh Bread, Destiny Image Fiction, and Treasure House books are available
at Christian bookstores and distributors worldwide.

1 2 3 4 5 6 7 8 9 10 / 09 08 07 06 05 04

For a U.S. bookstore nearest you, call
1-800-722-6774.
For more information on foreign distributors, call
717-532-3040.
Or reach us on the Internet:
www.destinyimage.com

Endorsements

God could not have given me a more beloved and effective "father" in ministry than Steve Crosby. He is the most thought-provoking, biblically literate individual I have ever known, and now Steve Crosby's internal dialogue is in print for the rest of the Church to benefit. Steve's prescription for performance-based religion is vintage Steve Crosby. He'll sober you up just in time to persuade you to become intoxicated with the true Gospel. I must warn you though! What you are about to read will forever change your perspective about relating to God. If you like your religion neatly organized and controllable then don't even open the following pages. Every Christian and those "burned" by religion should read this book.

Bob Grimm
Pastor, Christian Life Center
Walla Walla, Washington

Freedom! Dr. Crosby has written a book destined to liberate young and old alike who have unknowingly been shackled by rules and regulations void of the relational power of the Gospel. Subtle legalism within the Church drains us of the incredible life Christ offers us, leaving us hopeless, confused, and frustrated with Christianity as we know it. This book provides insight for living a life immersed in the unfathomable hope and grace of Jesus. Expect to be different after reading this book.

Dr. Crosby is an anointed preacher, powerful communicator, biblical theologian, and a prolific author. Beyond these, he is a spiritual father and one whom I respect very dearly. I endorse this book wholeheartedly as I believe the spirit of God will bring freedom to those desperately longing for a fresh glimpse into the heart of Christ.

Isaac Stokes, D.Min.
Author of: *After My Father's Heart*

I was challenged as I read The *Silent Killers of Faith* to think about my life and my 40 plus years of ministry and to reflect upon those areas of my life where the subtleties of legalism have raised their ugly head and sought to control. Thank you, Steve, for the reminder that our life in Christ and our relationship to His Body, the Church, is all about grace!

Al Woods, D.Min.
Senior Pastor, Door of Hope Church
Fairbanks, Alaska

In this insightful book, Dr. Crosby targets the prime enemy to our freedom in Christ…an enemy that has existed since Paul addressed the Galatian church. In sync with what the Holy Spirit is saying, Dr. Crosby deftly reveals the insidious effects of legalism. Perhaps more importantly, after revealing the prison legalism becomes, he shows us the way out! A freedom and sonship based solely on a love relationship with a personal Savior! Come discover how this barrier to our purpose and joy creeps into our life. Then, enjoy a new day freed from its prison. This book is a must-read for those longing to live in the real freedom Christ died to give us!

Lon Stokes
Pastor, Generational Ministries
Spokane, Washington

Acknowledgments

I am who I am today by the grace of God and the impartation of so many wonderful believers in the Lord's Church. It has been such a blessing to have had the life-enriching experience of having the highest quality individuals impart wisdom and encouragement into my life over 30 years of Christian experience. Should I start to mention names, I would undoubtedly omit someone who deserves recognition. So, I would like to thank my "families" by geography. Some people are fortunate to have one family. I am blessed with several.

To all my family and friends in:

—Sayre, Pennsylvania; Waverly, New York; and Elmira, New York

—Christian Life Center, in Walla Walla, Washington

—Generational Ministries Fellowship

—New Life Covenant Church in Wasilla, Alaska

—Door of Hope Network of Churches

I thank you.

And to Rita, my wife, whose rock-solid faith and steady partnership I have never taken for granted. I frequently marvel at the Lord's goodness to me, that I should be married to such a woman.

Table of Contents

Foreword

I haven't read this book! I don't have to! I have lived within the framework of the author's theology for the past six years. I have the advantage of having had relational trust built with Steve Crosby through pastoring, eldering, ministering, and relating as an associate and friend. Our destinies are woven together. Does this mean I'm not objective? I hardly think so. I can be his harshest critic. I know him, where he lives and what he believes. My prayer is that as you read this book you, too, will get to know this man, his theology, and his heart.

Steve preaches the cross of Christ applied to your life. It is only through the application of the cross of Christ to your life that you will be able to set aside your personal doctrines, phobias, and religious habits and hear the message of "Freedom from Religion" that Steve Crosby teaches. I know—I've had my heart changed through his teaching, and my future has been re-directed by it.

I will be eternally thankful for Steve's ability to communicate this much-needed truth to the Body of Christ. I trust that you will see it, hear it, want it, and live it. Read this book, open your heart then let Christ crucify it, and experience Kingdom freedom now!

John Yost
Pastor, Elder, Husband, Father, Alaskan bush pilot,
and all-around normal human male.

Introduction

Like a favorite pair of well-worn shoes, Christianity suited Stan. For over 20 years, he had enjoyed the best and adapted to the worst that local church life could offer. Neither embittered nor self-righteous, he embodied many genuine Christian virtues. His faithful ministry ranged from mop slinging to soul tending—a proverbial pillar of the church. Yet, in the beginning of his faith, an unrecognized tare had been sown, which ultimately grew to consume the entire field. An invisible power slowly worked incremental death in his spirit. Harvest time beckoned.

Stan's home church emphasized a message of Christian maturity. By his strength of character, sheer determination, and strong desire to please, Stan was productive in his environment. Peers and superiors recognized his efforts. However, his kingdom labors were unsatisfying. In spite of his diligence, an abiding sense of personal failure and inadequacy plagued Stan. At the end of each day, a subtle voice echoed in his soul. He sensed that his labors were meaningless, that he had fallen short of the standard expected of him. In the quiet moments of self-reflection, Stan felt as if he were a walking dead man.

Like a dancing dog in a variety show, his kingdom service had taken on a counterfeit quality. He could produce Christian behavior on demand in response to appropriate stimuli. Stan had learned obedience, but at the price of his identity. The exercise of responsibility and duty had swallowed the life of the Spirit in him.

Stan struggled in the most basic life functions. The simplest tasks, natural or spiritual, took inordinate energy. Every week Stan confessed his attitudes and rehearsed his failures (imagined or genuine) before the Lord—weeping, begging for rescue. The cavalry never appeared on the horizon. Rather, the gap between how he *should* feel and how he *did* feel widened. Stan slowly began to sink into a pool of cynicism and resentment against his calling, against God, and against God's leaders who, in Stan's eyes, began to appear duplicitous: purveyors of numbing and delusional doctrines for a congregation of pretenders. The emperor had no clothes, or so Stan thought.

Recognizing his dire condition, Stan reached out for help. He joined the men's accountability group looking for answers in the companionship of fellow travelers. Rather than finding answers, Stan's experience resembled a tax cheat's thrill knowing he has a weekly appointment with an IRS auditor. The routine of rigorous introspection and self-measurement only deepened his despair.

Since the problem could not be God's, it must be his. Stan eventually despaired of life and contemplated suicide. This drove him more deeply into condemnation, self-hate, and depression because, *as we all know,* such thoughts are inappropriate for Christians. Friends and leaders attempted to help him by exhorting him to obey the principles of God's Word, but a heavier load only expedites the collapse of a weakened bridge. After years of unuttered inward struggle, Stan had a nervous breakdown and was institutionalized.

Shocked church members now mention Stan's name in the hushed tones used when speaking of the dead. Suppressed embarrassment abounds. Eyes glance nervously at the floor. Feet shuffle uncomfortably. Minutes turn into hours. Stan's collapse exposed individual foundational flaws. "If someone as spiritual as Stan can collapse, what about me?" "What hope do I have?" "Does Christianity really work when you need it to?"

Stan's version of Christianity looked "right." The message he believed was biblical in content. His intentions were pure. Yet in the end, Stan found this "Christianity" ungratifying and lifeless. Something was terribly wrong. Deep in the foundations of his soul and in his understanding of Christianity, Stan had embraced an incorrect God image and a flawed Gospel.

I wish this story was entirely fictional. It is not. Stan is a composite character pieced together from the lives of innumerable individuals I have ministered to over the years.

Introduction

A subtle and silent killer flows in the life stream of the Body of Christ—a virus of devilish design and effectiveness. This masquerader promises life, but provides only death. Sweet to the mouth but bitter to the belly, it is the Venus flytrap of the kingdom, sending out promising fragrances, only to devour those who succumb to its allure. Like a stealth bomber or hypertension, it avoids detection until the damage is done. Preying on the weak and strong alike, it effectively neutralizes thousands of unaware believers. Its discreet presence belies its leavening permeation, devastating individuals, families, local churches, and ultimately the Gospel. What is this silent killer? *Legalism.*

Legalism is like spiritual halitosis: The other person has the bad breath problem, not me! The church down the road has a *major* issue, not *my* church...we are not under the law...we are Abraham's children...the seed of promise...we have the covenant...we are not in bondage. Sounds like another group of conservative, biblical literalists whose self-diagnosis of their freedom was erroneous when Jesus had the nerve to declare that they were slaves. (See John 8.)

The taproot of legalism runs deep in humanity. Its fountainhead is in Adam and it flows freely in us all. Trust in our correctness on certain theological tenets, precepts, and points of view, and a commitment to biblical conservatism does not automatically immunize us. Rather, without the *experiential reality* of the Person of Christ administered to us by the Holy Spirit, we will be perfect incubators for legalist infection. It is possible to be completely loyal to Paul's doctrine and know nothing of Paul's life: the curse of arid evangelicalism.

We all have a resident Pharisee within. Whether he politely minds his business with clean hands and a manicured life or trashes the place in drunken disregard makes no difference. He signed a lease in Adam and must be evicted. As Walt Kelly's comic strip character, Pogo, said: "We have met the enemy, and he is us." This book is not about pointing a finger at others. It is about cleaning the mirror.

This book has two thrusts: diagnosis and remedy. I hope to:

- expose legalism, the instigating spirit, in all its nuances;
- expose performance-based religion, the outcome or product of legalism;
- immunize believers who are unaffected by legalism and its progeny;

- and redeem those who have been ravaged by both.

I beg stylistic indulgence. I will use the terms *legalism* and *performance-based religion* interchangeably. Although legalism and performance-based religion do indeed have a cause-and-effect relationship, the line between the two blurs at times. At the real life level, the distinction might be of little practical value anyway. I have also taken stylistic license in not capitalizing references to satan or the devil as a means of not giving him honor or significance equal to our Lord. May He have preeminence in all things!

Po-"tay"-to: Po-"tah"-to

An Islamic terrorist and an American could sit at a table in The Hague discussing the mutual value and benefit of peace. After considerable negotiation, an agreement could be reached where both promised to amend their behavior to promote peace. Upon returning home, the Islamic terrorist would have no problem developing expanded strategies for attacks on the United States. We would exclaim: "Hypocrite!" "Liar!" "Deceiver!" But are those terms accurate and appropriate in this case? *Not necessarily.*

The problem lies in the definition of peace. To one party, peace is the absence of armed conflict. To another, peace is the removal of obstacles to Islamic subjugation of the world. *(Islam* means "submission" to Allah.) For Christians, peace on earth is the removal of enmity between God and humanity. For Muslims, it is the removal of unbelieving humanity with enmity; therefore, armed conflict that achieves the goal of subduing the nations to Allah secures peace. Non-Muslims are considered warmongers because their very existence hinders peace, as Muslims define it. The problem is definition influenced by culture, values, and worldview. We still do not get it.

The same is true of legalism in the universal Church and at the local church level.

DON'T TRUST THE LABEL

Scripture does not present legalism to us vacuum-packed with a list of ingredients on the wrapper. It does refer to being "under the law" (or not). What does that mean? For some, it is simply a matter of the Christian's non-relationship to the ceremonial laws of the Jews. It is considered impossible for a Christian to be a legalist since we are, *de facto,*[1] under grace. This belief is correct in the sense of the believer's standing or position in the Lord. We are not under the law as a sphere of relationship, government, or authority. However, it is not true in the sense of how someone might behave or think. I can be in the pew every Sunday, yet be a thoroughgoing legalist in relationship to God and humanity. I may be in grace, but grace may not be in me.

The *de facto* view contends that since the **specifics** (disputes concerning ritual observance, circumcision, holy days, dietary laws, etc.) encountered by Paul in Galatia and the other first century churches no longer exist (having been theologically dealt with) that the **problem** of legalism no longer exists either. Thank God the apostles dealt with those issues! However, the first century specifics were merely the vehicle used to import a more sinister toxic cargo into the Church. The philosophic cargo remains the same today though the delivery system has changed. The devilish goal is to supplant the preeminence of Christ and the reality of the Holy Spirit in the Church—by any and all means.

Satan is still running a black market smuggling business. He doesn't import legalism into the Church with a warning label: "Danger: Legalism enclosed. May be harmful to your health. Consume at your own risk!" If he keeps the cargo from being recognized, what difference does it make if he uses a '54 Chevy or 2004 Acura for delivery? We could post a 24-hour guard on bay 14 with this assignment: "Don't let any '54 Chevys near this dock, bless God!" All the while, the devil easily unloads his legalistic cargo on bay 25, simply because it is pleasantly gift-wrapped, untruthfully identified, and in a shiny new Acura.

The philosophical cargo matters, not the delivery system. Today's delivery system may be different from the Judaizing vehicle of Paul's day, but the devil's smuggling business is alive and profitable.

WHEN IN ROME, DO AS THE ROMANS DO

In our culture, the above cliché means a person should adapt to one's surroundings, culture, and customs when visiting another country. This quote is from Patristic literature. It was the advice given by the Church Fathers to Christians who asked how they should behave when visiting a church that did not share the same practices as their own.

Every local church has its own distinctives, emphases, and calling. These are the sovereign choices of the Holy Spirit—wonderful to behold and a participatory joy. However, each local church often has *unspoken* expectations of how a Christian should "behave." They are those values and practices, not biblically explicit, which for better or worse are expected of individuals in the local congregation. It is the consensus behavioral orthodoxy incorporated in local church vision and values, reinforced by leadership teaching, and practiced by core constituents. I call this phenomenon church culture. For instance, you may visit a church for the first time in a suit and tie and discover that the locals are very informal in their dress. In a relatively benign way, you have just experienced *church culture*. Not all experiences are equally as benign.

Frequently, the manifestation of church culture variations are not in the realm of right and wrong, sin or not sin. They are the gray areas where only secondary and inferential arguments can be made from Scripture. For example, Scripture clearly speaks about honor and modesty. It says less about how honor is to manifest itself in a Sunday dress code! If a local assembly feels strongly on a church culture matter, the local terminology will be expressed in terms of "convictions." Those who deviate from or are dispassionate toward the convictions will be accepted as fellow believers, but not as fully part of the "vision of the house." If sentiments toward a church culture matter are less strong, they will be expressed in terms of "custom" or "practice," and they will not be used to define someone's status in the local assembly. It normally does not take too long to discover which is which. Church culture strongly affects one's view and definition of legalism.

Within any virtue are the seeds of self-distortion. A church culture may reflect emphasis on a legitimate biblical virtue. However, if pushed to an extreme, or if held apart from the revelation of grace and the reality of the Spirit, the virtue becomes a vice. The unique quality distinguishing the fellowship becomes the seedbed of legalism. How?

- Honesty becomes brutality.

- Thriftiness becomes miserliness.

- Compassion becomes enabling.

- Courage becomes insensitivity.

- Sensitivity becomes sentimentality.

- Integrity becomes superiority.
- Destiny becomes self-centeredness.
- Conviction becomes inflexibility.
- Flexibility becomes vacillation.

Are You in the Zoo?

Once a dominant ethos is established in a church culture, it is often cultivated, consciously or not, by behavioral rules, expectations, and accountability programs. Rather than being considered legalism, the accountability ethos of the group is viewed as those reasonable behavioral expectations that maintain core values and identify individuals as members of the group. We don't _____ or we do _____ because... (You can fill in the blanks!) For instance, a group whose emphasis is Christian maturity or integrity can succumb to behavior codes and accountability believed necessary to maintain corporate and individual integrity. Likewise, a group whose emphasis is compassion will develop a church culture that rewards behaviors consistent with the core value and discourages those that seem opposed to it.

External accountability is like driving with the sheriff in the backseat of your car. As long as the sheriff is there, no one is going to speed! Remove the external presence of authority and a speeder is reborn! It is a mistake to think that persisting in accountability long enough will produce a change of nature. Rather, a change of nature will produce accountability.

Accountability only enables performance-based religion. It is the self-aware, self-monitoring Adamic counterfeit of biblical discipleship. It is like a zookeeper who expects the cage to change a tiger into a pussy-cat. The bars only *restrain* the tiger. Take away the bars and what do you have? Tiger, and lots of it! However, if the tiger's nature was somehow changed, the bars would no longer be necessary. This is exactly what *should* experientially happen for believers: Rebels are supposed to have been made into obedient children. A new nature is supposed to have been imparted at salvation.

Sometimes our conversion and sanctification experience have all the spiritual vitality of a freeze-dried TV dinner. Because we are weak, the Church often embraces accountability as a means of keeping the unregenerate Adamic nature in check! *We try to sanctify people who have not experienced a genuine change of nature,* or who are *experientially out of touch* with their new nature. This is particularly true for second and third generation children who have grown up in the church. Sure, our children may have said the sinner's prayer when they were six years old, but somewhere along the way, the experiential reality of regeneration is lost. Rather, they have figured out, embraced, and conformed to the church culture and its expectations.

Our churches are full of frustrated tigers and exhausted zookeepers who resort to the whip of legalism and accountability (most of the time unconsciously) as the only thing they know to keep the tiger in check! Eventually the cage and whip will destroy the animal's essential nature. It will just lay in the back of the cage in a lethargic stupor. Its outward presence says animal, but its inward essence has been destroyed. Often the zookeeper no longer uses the whip to *restrain* wild behavior; now he has to use it to get *any* response from the animal.

Spiritual sons and daughters who become exhausted from fighting against the external restraints of legal accountability eventually just give up. Their essential nature is so crushed that they simply collapse into the church culture and its accountability system. "Fine, whatever it is that you want, I will give it to you. Just lay off the whip, will you?" Passivity and withdrawal set in.

In a spiritual climate where passivity has taken root, it is futile to try to get production from lethargic believers. You can bark motivational slogans like a Marine drill sergeant all day long with little result. The unenlightened drill sergeants will not understand why their accountability partners or protégés lay motionless in the back of their spiritual cages, or merely yawn at the proposition of actually moving forward. *They do not realize that the essential nature has been destroyed!* The whip of accountability and the mantras of the high calling cannot awaken an exhausted son or daughter—only a healed identity can.

All restraints, codes, and principles of accountability are impotent to change the nature of the one in the cage. In fact, the tiger will resent the cage because it conflicts with his essentially wild nature. He may obediently pace the perimeter of the cage, staying within its boundaries, but he is really checking for weakness because the artificial environment does not suit his wild and free nature. Likewise, the bars of accountability on a Spirit-son of the New Covenant will ultimately lead either to resentment toward the bars and the one who put them there, or to disengaged passivity. ***Obedience gained on the altar of conformity to church culture is a legal abomination.***

Now, of course, a caged tiger is better than a loose one prowling the neighborhood! Likewise, accountability is better than unbridled sin, but the manifestation of the life of the Son is *much* better than policed accountability. Being accountable does indeed restrain the carnal nature, but it takes constant diligence and effort to see that the cage is properly maintained. Any detected weakness must immediately be reinforced by more bars, more rules. A patrolling zookeeper is required to inspect the condition of the cage and the behavior of the animal.

To some people, the "zookeeper and tiger-in-the-cage scenario" is biblical accountability, but I call it bondage. I am through with the zoo. I returned my zookeeper's union card.

DON'T CALL US; WE'LL CALL YOU

Some leaders mistakenly view any shred of initiative or ambition in a subordinate as a manifestation of the Adamic nature. Docility is viewed as a virtue. Passivity is considered Christ-like. I have heard it said that anyone who expresses interest in leadership (as in the office of an elder/bishop) automatically proves he is not qualified because ambition is carnal. Disinterest is considered a fruit of the Spirit.

However, Scripture says that *someone who desires* (stretches out, reaches for, grasps, extends, gives everything for) *the office of leadership* (elder, bishop) *desires a good thing!* (See 1 Timothy 3:1.) Church culture says: Be polite; don't put yourself forward; let the Holy Spirit decide those things, etc.

I know of a wise pastor who once had a young man come to him in all sincerity and say, "Pastor, I want to be a minister. Will you please help me?" The pastor could have lectured the young man and told him about submission, how inappropriate it is to put himself forward, how he needs to learn to serve another first, how he needs to sit for a season, how God must prepare him, etc. Instead, the pastor excitedly said, "Yes, I would love to train you!" He immediately took the young man's hand, led him to the janitorial closet, handed him a mop and said, "Start ministering," then walked away. In a simple, yet dynamic and profound way, that pastor *affirmed* the young man's *desire* and led him to Calvary at the same time!

IGOR, BRING ME A HEART

In Mary Shelley's classic novel *Frankenstein,* the good Dr. Frankenstein fastened together bits and pieces of what *used to be* alive on others, manipulated a source of power (lightning), and created a distorted form of life. In Christian circles, accountability programs frequently become a distortion of a genuine biblical virtue: a father-son, discipling relationship.[2] Dr. Adam-stein tries to produce a son from the bits and pieces of what died in the garden, charges it with an artificial legal principle (responsible Christian behavior), and the result is a Franken-son.

We get it backward. We expect accountability to produce sons. Accountable behavior will never produce a father-son relationship; rather, a father-son relationship spontaneously begets accountable behavior. Jesus was not a Son because He behaved. He behaved because He was a Son. His identity was the basis of His actions. Accountability is similar to authority—it is something that can be offered freely, but not demanded. Accountability is the freewill offering of a crucified son-heart. Promoting accountability in an individual without a crucified son-heart, merely encourages Cain to gain from his labors, the behavioral acceptance only death and resurrection can produce. Obedient hearts beget accountability; accountability never produces obedient hearts.

The means for preventing the virtue-to-vice slide is not found in the limits of man-made behavioral boundaries—acceptable and unacceptable codes of conduct. It is in the revelational reality of the indwelling Christ, the manifest reality of His Spirit, and the power of His cross at work in the lives of believers. Anyone can design an accountability form and require others to submit it weekly. It is another matter altogether to be an incarnation of the life of God in the earth, possessing the substance of the Son of God within, giving it freely to others.

LEGALISM AND HOLINESS

Church culture also has a profound influence on the question of what is holy and what is legal. For example:

- *One person's holiness is another's bondage.*

  My daughter's dress must be three inches *below* the knee, but your daughter's is an inch and a half *above.* Somebody is a compromiser and we cannot fellowship together.

- *One's conviction is another's intolerance.*

  You do not believe women should have authority, so you will never submit to a female civil judge. My wife is on the circuit court of appeals. Somebody is a compromiser and we cannot fellowship with each other.

- *One's liberty is another's license.*

  I will watch a violent R-rated movie, and you will watch only G-rated movies.[3]

- *One's diligence is another's slavery.*

  I have 15-minute devotions twice a day: the morning and evening sacrifice. You only pray twice a week for two hours.

- *One's purity is another's prudishness.*

  I believe women should be covered from nose to toes. You think neck to knee is good enough. Somebody is….ah, I think you've got it.

All these simplistic dualities are fertile ground for latent legalism and are not too distant from common realities in a local church. The problem is: Who defines what is holy and what is legal?

Holiness that leads to *isolation* or *insulation* is a biblical counterfeit. Religion without love has been responsible for most of the world's misery. A.W. Tozer said, "You can find more carnal, unregenerate, self-centered characters in the church who have religion and are sensitive toward it than you can bury in the Grand Canyon."[4] Separation that begets a spirit of superiority is a betrayal of Christ and His Gospel. A commitment to excellence and spiritual maturity that cannot accommodate weakness and immaturity in others is high-octane fuel for the engine of legalism.

GROWN UP OR WORN OUT?

Maturity. Is there a more dangerous Christian concept? How many thousands of believers have been brought into the bondage of legalistic slavery under the guise of progressing to spiritual maturity?

At the beginning of our Christian walk, we first hear the good news of the Gospel and are convinced that there is nothing we can do to help ourselves, other than to believe and accept God's offer (His grace and salvation). Later, post conversion, all of a sudden it is up to *us* to *do* something, to produce this thing called "Christian maturity." The "should do and should not do" list descends on the new convert like a lead blanket, weighing down the nascent life of God with the duties of responsible Christian living. Often the rank heathen have a more genuine Gospel hope than the sons and daughters of the house. It seems I am saved freely, but it is all up to me after that. Rather than initiation into the realities of life in the Spirit and an experiential relationship with the living Lord in the power of resurrected life, new converts are conditioned and conformed to church culture.

Mentors with empty canteens cannot offer water to others. They can only invite the new convert to join them—lock-stepping in the footprints left by other thirsty, parched, and dying hikers who trudged their way through the Sahara of performance-based religion required by church culture, only to collapse at the pearly gates and have Saint Peter drag them in.

I know of a situation where the wife of a young couple with leadership potential was given a 40-page instruction manual on how to be an elder's wife! *Forty, 8 ½ by 11-inch pages!* The apostle Paul only presented a very abbreviated list of requirements for leadership in two places in Scriptures, yet the church somehow needs 40 pages of instruction on the subject. No legalism at work there, just developing responsible Christian maturity. Uh-huh.

I am not implying that sanctification is not important. It is *how* one is sanctified that is critical. Indeed, a good planting produces good fruit. The key is a change of life source, not effort in fruit production (more about this in later chapters).

When we allow "things," even *good* things, to define church culture rather than the liberating Spirit of Christ—presented in the power of the New Covenant and in the manifestation of the Holy Spirit—we have established a legal atmosphere. A wag once said that some people's religion is like a wooden leg: There is neither warmth nor life in it and although it helps you to hobble along, it never becomes part of you—you must strap it on every morning.

It is possible to win a point of argument yet, all the while, betray the Spirit of Christ and be more legal than the one whom you may "defeat" with your reasoning. I may win the point of doctrine technically but lose the life-giving Spirit. If I am outside the Spirit, I am in the law. For many, whether or not something is "legal" (or holy) is all about externals. Is the hair up or down? (my grandparent's generation)…is it too long? (my generation)…or too short and with a tattoo? (current generation)…seems like the Church just cannot get enough of this one. Whatever the issues, they are symptomatic of a deeper philosophical worldview, psychological state, mindset, and relationship to God.

SETTING THE NAIL

Legalism is more than external rule observance or non-observance. It is a system of thought, an approach to life and life's God. It is the belief that one's personal character and holiness grants special and intimate access to God's presence and blessings, thereby establishing oneself as superior to other believers. The legalist says, "My acceptance and advance in God is contingent upon, or improved by, my behavior." Good behavior earns me more of God's favor, which in turn impels me to higher levels of spiritual life—"the next level." God's love is conditioned on the legalist's performance. A legalist's God rewards (blesses) for good behavior but punishes for bad. Legalists will be obsessively introspective, self-centered, and manic in "trying to please God." Taken up with the shine and maintenance of their vessels, legalists will be blindingly indifferent to the need and plight of others around them.

Legalism believes that God's grace is a kind of divine public assistance plan, provided by the Father and subscribed to by humanity because it is weak. Grace is the spiritual coupon I cash in when I have run out of my own resources. God forbid! We are not just weak in Adam—we are dead in Adam, disqualified in Adam. And we do not need a little help from a heavenly welfare agency. We need, and—praise be to God—have been freely given, a completely new life source!

Sanctification…holiness…spiritual maturity (or whatever one wants to call it) results as life is yielded to, not as achievement is attained. Spiritual advancement in God's Kingdom is a death-resurrection process, not a spiritual housekeeping process. The extension of His life in me, and in the world, is not related to how well I can adorn myself with spiritual virtues. It is about the death I am willing to embrace that His life might be made manifest through me, at all times, in all places, under all circumstances.

Any thought, action, or deed that has its source outside of Christ and Him crucified, outside of His life within us, is fundamentally legalistic. Any philosophy, biblical or otherwise, any behavior, noble or ignoble, that supplants the place and preeminence of Christ and the reality of the Holy Spirit is fundamentally legalistic. It is contrary to the New Covenant Gospel of grace which should be preached with power and illumined by the Holy Spirit.

Definition is EVERYTHING!

CHAPTER ONE

End Notes

1. *De facto* means: As a self-evident reality; "the way it is" that needs little or no explanation.

2. No gender specificity is implied.

3. One of the most disturbing, defiling movies I have ever seen was a G-rated flick from a rodent-based, animation outfit in central Florida. More poison and spiritual death was sweetly packaged in that movie than in any number of other films that I have seen that were R-rated because of violence. Simply because people keep their clothes on, don't swear, and don't shoot anybody doesn't mean it is automatically a "safe" or godly movie! Only a legalist would think so.

4. A.W. Tozer quoted in Blanchard, John *Gathered Gold*, (HeretFordshire: Evangelical Press, 1984) p. 261.

Root and Fruit

A seed of performance-based religion was sown in humanity in the Garden of Eden and has been composted well in the Church since the days of the Apostles. It took root in Adam and blossoms regularly in his descendants like crocuses in spring, generation after generation. Legalism is like hybrid wheat. You can call it "quick grow," "high yield," "disease resistant," "winter wheat," or whatever. It is essentially…wheat! Legalism has many forms, but the essential nature has not changed since the dawn of creation.

To understand how legalism manifests in the Church today, it will be helpful to examine its beginnings—root and first fruit. Genesis reveals the root, Galatians the fruit. We will examine Galatians in more detail in Chapters Eight and Nine.

WHAT'S LOVE GOT TO DO WITH IT?

The drama surrounding the tree of the knowledge of good and evil often distracts from the fact that there were *two* trees in the midst of the garden: the tree of the knowledge of good and evil *and* the tree of life (see Gen. 2:9). Obviously, Adam and Eve were presented with alternatives from the beginning. Satan distorted God's prohibition, implying a ban on access to the tree of life (see Gen. 3:1); Eve embraced the distortion and added to it (see Gen. 3:3). She accepted a mischaracterization of God's nature and intent. She distorted what God said by adding on a requirement: Don't touch it. God never said, "Don't touch it." He said, "Don't eat from it" (see Gen. 2:16-17).

Why would God purposefully create this situation where both trees were accessible, where temptation could occur with such cosmically disastrous consequences? The prohibition against eating from the tree of the knowledge of good and evil was not a divine set-up trying to trick Adam and Eve into sinning. God knew that partaking of the tree would be to their hurt. The taboo was a *parental* form of love expressed as a desire to protect from harm. Parent-child love, while warm and affectionate, has an unmistakable quality of authority with it.

Soldiers who pass through combat together often form a bond of love that is life long. The love bond is formed because of joint participation in an action. Creator-creation love is similar. It is valuable and genuine, yet take away the bonding experience and would love exist?

God's purpose in providing an opportunity for choice between two trees goes beyond parental or creator-creation love. He was trying to draw out a deeper form of love from Adam and Eve than parent-child, or creator-creation love. He was attempting to establish a relational love based on individualized personhood and identity: in type, husband-wife love. *God wanted relationship with Adam and Eve based on their value and desire of Him in His Personhood, not His authority, nor His creative might. Love* **required** *two trees.*

To many Christians, God's love is a theological abstraction with little psychological and emotional reality. Although care must be taken not to anthropomorphize God (gain understanding by ascribing to Him merely magnified human qualities), somehow, without the corruption of sin or without any personal lack, God has capacity for love and love is based on desire. God is, after all, holy love.

Although God is not merely a bigger version of humanity, neither is He as Hollywood would have us believe, characterized as "the Force"—an impersonal but almighty abstraction who exists to be manipulated by the enlightened and initiated, a divine power supply to tap into when we see fit. He has full Personhood.

Our desires are rooted in lack. We lack money, we lack a mate, we lack a home, and our desire is extended to meet our need. Because God lacks nothing, His desire is not lack or need-based. To think the Almighty possesses uncontaminated, holy desire is hard for us to grasp. However, our corrupted emotions are the only point of psychological reference we have as we try to describe the indescribable. Again, in some way transcending all our understanding of what it means to have perfected Personhood, God possesses perfected desire.

The two trees were required because God desired to be desired. Would His creation love Him freely? Would He be valued in His Personhood? Desire cannot be expressed in an atmosphere where choice is impossible, where value does not exist, and where risk cannot happen. In order to love fully, one must allow the possibility of rejection—the expression of "disvalue." Love says: "I choose you over another. I desire you, as you, over all others." In a choice-less atmosphere, obedience can exist—the obedience of children, servants, robots, or drones—but love is impossible.

If I was on a deserted island with only one available member of the opposite sex, there would technically be freedom of choice, but no possibility of making a genuine selection based on desire. If option B does not exist, choosing option A is not necessarily love. Such a choice is desire-less. It is a default selection. If my love is based on self-interest and self-gratification at the expense of the other party, rather than recognition of value in the other, my love is not love at all, but an ugly form of self-gratification that uses the other person to satisfy my own needs.

For example the answer to many men's (to a lesser extent, women's) pornography addiction, or lustful thought life, is dealing with the root of self-centeredness, not lust. There is no emotional cost with pornography. I do not have to extend value to another human being, but can take all the satisfaction I can get. The ancient Greeks had a symbol for self-centered, sexual (*eros*) love. It was a picture of a snake swallowing its own tail— complete self-absorption to the point of self-destruction. Take care of self-centeredness, and lust will go away rather easily. Clean up the garbage in the alley and the rats leave.

In the marital union, two individuals come together and share a new life. God's desire for Adam and Eve was to participate with Him in His life and love. He desired a creation suited for Himself, someone with whom He could exchange love based on desire, a creation fit for Himself, bearing His image, just as Eve was suited for Adam.[1] Unfortunately, they chose another avenue. The tree of knowledge was seen as desirable, not God in His Personhood (see Gen. 3:6). Adam and Eve did not just make a disobedient behavioral decision. They made a value judgment: "God, You are not desirable. We choose enlightenment and power without You, over life and love with You." Humanity's fall is not merely about disobedient children and their punishment, nor a creation gone awry like an engine that has thrown a bearing. It is about love lost.

The admonition against eating the forbidden fruit bothered me for many years. In some ways, it seemed a petty thing. The spiritual significance of "the day you eat you will surely die" was obviously vast. That did not bother me. Why the admonition about *eating*? Why did God put the admonition in terms of eating or not eating instead of saying, "Don't embrace this philosophy," or "Don't live this way," or "Don't listen to the serpent"?

To eat something is to have it transformed to become part of you. It is not merely putting food in your mouth and swallowing it. For instance, what goes in my mouth as steak is transformed by my metabolic processes into the flesh of Steve Crosby (and what an all too efficient process it is at times!). In time and space, the steak has *literally* taken on a new dimension and expression as the result of being consumed. At one time, the steak was limited to being a cow, but now it is I! The admonition against eating the fruit of the tree of the knowledge of good and evil was not an arbitrary command concerning not eating fruit. God was saying that the tree of the knowledge of good and evil was not to have a transformed and expanded expression in God's creation. As explained above, its presence was required as the necessity of love, but God was opposed to giving it incarnated expression. By eating of it, Adam and Eve gave incarnation to what was previously only a potentiality.

BLAME IT ON THE WOMAN

Humanity's fall is commonly considered to be "Eve's failure." However, although Eve is "in Adam" in a collective sense of humanity (see Gen. 2:23; 5:2), the Scripture calls the matter, *Adam's* sin. She may have been deceived, but Adam was disobedient (see 1 Tim. 2:14; Rom. 5:19). Eve was duped, but Adam knew what he was doing. Genesis 3:6 states clearly that Adam was "with her." He was there for the whole transaction with the serpent, but said and did nothing. There is no place for gender superiority when it comes to vulnerability to legalism. Adam and Eve were in cahoots together. It was a tag team effort: a blind woman and a cowardly man.

Male silence and inactivity in the face of crisis or decision is as old as the Garden. Adam did not want to risk rejection from Eve. Many damaged men vainly try to gain a sense of identity from the women in their lives rather than from the Father in their lives. It is a tragic mistake played out in the lives of thousands. A woman can give a man of lot of things, but identity and psychological wholeness are not among them.

IT'S ALL IN YOUR HEAD

There has been some confusion on the matter of the knowledge of good and evil. Some believe that the ban on eating from the tree of the knowledge of good and evil means believers should not even exercise intellectual differentiation between good and evil. Any moral exercise or intellectual endeavor involving a choice between good and evil is viewed as fundamentally flawed, of a lesser spiritual quality, a lower realm than the mystical life of the spirit we are allegedly promised from the tree of life.

This is problematic. Hebrews chapter 5 defines spiritual maturity as having our senses exercised to discern between good and evil. If mere intellectual ability to discern between good and evil is equivalent to living from the tree of knowledge, we are in trouble. The confusion exists because of a Western view of knowledge as intellectual apprehension of facts. The Semitic or Mediterranean (this would include Greek) understanding of knowledge did not consider it to be apprehension of facts. For Semites, knowledge included participation in, or with, the object of one's knowledge. Only when someone had participatory experience were they considered to have knowledge, and because of experience, their knowledge took on the quality of trustworthiness. Semitic and Greek values tend to be more interlocked than modern Western values. The space and scope of this writing prevents a detailed language and cultural excursion, but let me provide a simple analogy.

Imagine a pilot who graduated at the top of the class in flight school with a 4.0 grade point average, but who has actually never flown a plane. In a sense, he or she has knowledge, but you are not too keen about getting on the plane when that pilot is at the controls! Why? Their knowledge is *not trustworthy, because it is not experiential.* This captures the Semitic concept of knowledge. It is participatory and connected with trustworthiness.

Thus the knowledge and eating metaphor in Genesis is about giving expression to something, not simply having an intellectual understanding of something. Therefore, in both the image of eating and in the definition of knowledge itself, the admonition to Adam and Eve was not a prohibition against intellectual awareness. It was prohibition *against participation in a way, a method, or philosophy* other than the life of God.

The question every believer faces concerning his or her behavior is not, "Is this right or wrong?" It should be, "Is this life and love or is it death?" Jesus could be the friend of sinners. He could go where they went and fellowship with them. The devil had no root in Him and He brought life to every situation He touched. His behavior was not a decision about, "Should I or shouldn't I?" (the legalist's dilemma), but "What is My Father doing and what will bring life?" Jesus' conflict with the Judeans was always about life compared with right and wrong. Whether eating the wheat on the Sabbath or healing a blind man, He was brought into conflict with those whose concept of pleasing God was adherence to code and rules as compared to bringing life to the situation.

What has all this got to do with legalism? Simply put, legalism is the attempt by humanity to substitute living by the knowledge of good and evil for living by life and love. It is the difference between *knowing the Lord's Book* and *through the Book, knowing the Lord*. It is a prohibited philosophical worldview.

CRUSH IT IN THE CRADLE

It is easier to defeat something when it is small and without strength than when it is fully developed. It makes sense at a human, strategic, and tactical level and is one of the more prevalent devilish ploys in Scripture: destroy or corrupt something in its inception. If the seed can be corrupted, everything the seed reproduces will reflect the corruption; and, since reproduction is a process of multiplication, not merely addition (one seed produces more than one additional seed—it produces hundreds or thousands), corrupting the seed, in whatever form or arena of life, is the most effective strategy an enemy could develop.

The following passages are a few examples of assault on a seed. Each faced an attempt to destroy them, and God's mission through them, in the beginning, infancy, childhood, or youth:

- Adam and Eve (Gen. 2–3)

- The birth of Moses (Exod. 2:1-10)

- The birth of Jesus (Matt. 2:13-23)

- The temptation of Jesus (Luke 4:1-13)

- Saul of Tarsus (Acts 9:20-25)

- Israel as a nation (Exod. 14:14-31)

- The Man-child (Rev. 12:4-5)

- Joash (2 Kings 11)

- Joseph (Gen. 37:1-36)

- David (1 Sam. 18:10–20:15)

Dr. Nolan Ball of Panama City, Florida, has a great insight concerning the importance of a pure seed. Naturally speaking, a hybrid often tastes better, grows faster, and may look nicer than the original seed from which it was developed. However, a hybrid does not have within it the power to naturally reproduce. It must be artificially induced to produce.

Many things in the church may look successful by American values of success: size, money, influence, etc., but they do not have trans-generational power. Hybrid methodologies in the church—mixtures of ungodly/secular/worldly and Kingdom philosophies—may appear to give success in one generation, but true spiritual value will not be discernible until at least three generations (Abraham, Isaac, and Jacob) have passed and there is Kingdom increase. You cannot tell the value of the seed until harvesttime, and one generation is not Kingdom harvest.

Church growth statistics state that when church transfers are excluded from the data, the evangelical church *in America* (Thank God, revival is exploding in other parts of the world!) is experiencing overall decline. We are not even reaching and maintaining the faith of our children. There is something wrong in the seed, in spite of the size of our churches. God builds generationally by family, and any other method will have to be artificially induced in each generation to keep it alive.

God's command to Adam and Eve was to be fruitful, multiply, and fill the earth with a godly seed, thereby extending God's life and government in the earth. The increase of His government can only be accomplished generationally. The devil is entirely content to allow a single generation to come to great levels of success both numerically and qualitatively because he knows that if the foundational seed is corrupted, he will ultimately prevail. Patience and endurance seem to be more effectively practiced by the devil than by many American believers who expect success from clever methodology instead of a death and life process that might take years, if not generations. The devil has the skill of a prizefighter who knows that losing or winning a round or two does not determine the outcome of the fight. The church and individual believers are content with winning a round or two.

STRANGERS SOWING CORRUPT SEED

Legalism was the first theological salvo fired by the devil across the bow of the Early Church. Strangers from Jerusalem with appealing credentials (the nature of the appeal will be discussed in the next chapter) were bringing a doctrine into the church of Galatia that undermined Paul's apostolic doctrine and his fatherly relationship with the church. Paul personally birthed (planted, began) the congregation in Galatia. He, not others, had legitimate primary spiritual authority and relationship to the congregation. The intensely sincere individuals from Jerusalem could not lay claim to the relational connection. They were motivated from a basis of adherence to principles rather than life and relationship. From their sincere but misguided motivation, they attempted to import the values of the tree of the knowledge of good and evil into the congregation—and were close to succeeding. So much so, that the church was on the brink of abandoning not only Paul's teaching, but also Paul's fathering relationship. The Jerusalem "brothers" were strangers in the house, importing a "bad seed," and Paul responded to the situation by writing the letter we call the Book of Galatians.

According to what is called the South Galatia theory[2] Paul wrote Galatians around A.D. 49. Assuming (as I do) this is correct, Galatians is the earliest of Paul's letters and contemporary with the writing of Mark's Gospel. What is the significance? Only *16 years* after the Lord's resurrection, a corrupting influence was *already* working its way into the infant church. The devil was attempting to corrupt the foundational seed.

Persecution was the method the devil used from *outside* the church to crush it in the cradle. He used legalism and Gnosticism (a subject too broad for me to go into detail here) from *within* the church to the same end. Seed corruption was the strategy; legalism and Gnosticism were the tactics. In a simple way, they each represented two corrupting extremes: legalism the extreme of regimented performance-based religion and Gnosticism the extreme of libertinism.[3]

For the legalist, Christ and Him crucified was not enough for salvation, sanctification, and spiritual maturity. Other things were required to "please God" and to achieve Christian "fullness and maturity." For the legalist, salvation is Christ plus _____ (fill in with the duty of your choice).

For the Gnostic,[4] Christ was a phantom who did not actually appear in a literal, physical body—His body was an illusion. For a Gnostic, the physical realm was irrelevant to spiritual matters, therefore one could indulge the body in any way one desired—bodily discipline or indulgence were irrelevant in the Gnostic scheme of things.

In a backward sort of way, all this should encourage us! If a church that was planted and shepherded by the greatest apostle the Church has ever known, experienced an internal problem only *16 years* after the resurrection (eyewitnesses still living!) there is absolutely no grounds for spirits of shame, condemnation, or failure to settle on any of us! If we find ourselves as either part of the problem or responsible for trying to fix it in our churches, we are in some good company! Whether or not we have a legalism problem is not the issue. The question is, are we willing to respond *apostolically*, as Paul did, if at all? Do we share the same apostolic *perspective* and *passion* on the matter as the apostle Paul? Are we content to let the ship sail along "all is well," or are we willing to disrupt the Sunday morning pastoral dance party on deck five to apostolically deal with the rats in the hold?

RATS DON'T GO EASILY

The letter to the Galatians and the Corinthian epistles are Paul's most disciplinary letters (Galatians being the most rhetorically passionate of the three, with Second Corinthians coming across the line a close second). The Greek words and phrases Paul uses in Galatians are full of intense and highly charged emotional language. Beginning with the significant lack of an opening greeting[5] through the middle of chapter 5, the tone is cursing (not foul language, but cursing in a blessing-versus-cursing sense), confrontational, challenging, combative, militaristic, insulting, mocking, jeering, threatening—literally, one "in your face" statement after another. At approximately the middle of chapter 5, after he has exhausted himself with emotional intensity trying to get his point across, Paul changes to a more fatherly tone of identification, pleading, and entreaty. Then he finishes the letter quite abruptly with another dismissive remark and a *very nominal* (compare it to some of Paul's other letters) final blessing (see Gal. 6:17-18).

Generations of romanticizing and feminizing have distorted the biblical image of Christ. For many, Jesus is Mister Rogers with a beard: a kind and gentle man in a sweater who is no threat...no intensity of personality.[6] Jesus is the ultimate nice guy. However, as Philip Yancey says, "How would telling people to be nice to one another get a man crucified? What government would execute Mister Rogers or Captain Kangaroo?"[7] Because of centuries of this psychological conditioning, it may be difficult for the reader to believe what I say about Paul's passionate response to the encroachment of legalism. The scope of this writing prohibits a verse-by-verse exegetical study to prove my point, and we will look a bit more in detail in later chapters. For now, I strongly encourage the diligent student to do some original language work and verify that what I am saying is true.

Not only has our understanding of the Person of Christ been romanticized and feminized, but the definition of what constitutes Christ-like behavior has also been compromised by centuries of unbiblical representations. Lest the reader think I am about to launch into a stereotypical male diatribe against uppity women in the church (men rule, women drool), let me preface my comments. I am a biblical egalitarian. I believe the Galatians 3:28 mandate applies beyond men and women being "equally saved." I am theologically and exegetically convinced, from a conservative commitment to biblical integrity, that the post-Pentecost era is characterized by complete gender equality in ministry opportunity. Having said that, I probably have alienated half of you! However, I do believe the church suffers, from pulpit to pew, with overemphasis, imbalance, and dominance of a feminizing spirit—an exaltation of a feminized value system, worldview, and ministerial ethic.

Because of the bridal imagery used of the Church in Scripture, the receptive/passive attitude of the feminine principle is frequently perceived as the decisive, dominant, or distinguishing quality or grace of a Christian or Christianity, and the essential elements of Christian character are gentle mildness and passive receptivity. This stereotype has been fueled for centuries by romantic European art in which Jesus is portrayed with grotesquely sentimental female qualities. Henry Ward Beecher (an influential nineteenth-century American *Unitarian*) said that a *mother's* love is "a revelation of the love of God." Another Unitarian claimed that true Christianity involved the rejection of all that is masculine.[8]

To many, the ideal pastor or leader is a man who has female sensitivities packaged in the anatomy of a man! For many male unbelievers, the concept of going to church means leaving one's masculinity at the door and having to think, act, and feel like a woman in order to find acceptance. Is it any wonder that apart from a revival spirit, men, as a whole, do not want anything to do with what they see in Christianity?[9]

Whenever and wherever I may chair a men's group discussion, I like to do a little test. I ask those in attendance to make a list of "Christian" virtues. (*Before you read further make your own list and see how you test out!*) The results are typically weighted in favor of what could be called the feminine virtues of humility, gentleness, meekness, mercy, etc. The more masculine virtues of courage, boldness, confrontation, daring, warring, frankness, truth, honesty, holiness, ability to endure hardship, deprivation, and suffering, etc., are *always* in the minority, *if listed at all*.

In Paul's letter to the Galatians, he is manifesting the masculine anointing of God. Paul understood the seriousness of the doctrinal assault in its specifics and the principle of seed corruption. The future of the faith hinged on a doctrinal battle in a small church in Eurasia. It got Paul's dander up. He was not about to respond Adamically—do nothing and say nothing in the face of a threat—but rather the Christ within, the Second Adam made after Christ, arose in Paul and he responded with masculine strength and a fatherly spirit to defend the Lord's blind bride.

To help the reader process this potential paradigm shift, a very *brief* word study follows. It is an attempt to *biblically* define our terms. Definition is everything.

GENTLENESS, HUMILITY, AND MEEKNESS

It is important to distinguish genuine biblical Christianity from the Americanized counterfeit. A tendency exists within all of us to adapt the Scriptures to suit the sensibilities of our personality, upbringing, class, and culture.[10] Add a few stereotypical religious mindsets to the mix and the result will be a passionately defended mental stronghold with *no basis in biblical Christianity*. We frequently hold tighter to our understanding of God than to God's understanding (as revealed in Scripture). We tend to read what we believe rather than believe what we read.

Without interpretive diligence, culture and personal preference imperceptibly migrate into doctrine and dogma, becoming the pillars of a legalistic mental stronghold. Since the essence of idolatry is to form God after our own image and thought, it is important to understand what the Scriptures really mean, not what one might naturally gravitate to because of a specific translational rendering (for better or worse), cultural mores, or upbringing.

We *must start* our interpretation with what the original hearers understood, not with what the words have come to mean to us through our culture.

HUMILITY

(*Gr.* tapeinophrosúne)

There is hardly a more abused biblical term. Humility is frequently equated with a spineless, doormat-like, self-deprecating, self-aware, introspective, cautious, conservative spirit of inferiority. The Greek root word, *tapeinós*, connotes a groveling, slavish, cowardly servility. It was morally contemptible and almost universally interpreted negatively. Aristotle viewed it somewhat positively but admitted it was hard for men to be it. In classical Greek, humility (in the positive sense) was defined as modesty: an unassuming diffidence not unlike magnanimity (from a Greek word meaning largeness of soul). Many Christians would accept this definition as biblical humility. *It is not*. Magnanimity is *self-aware*. It does not include the concept of sin or of man's standing before a holy God. It is a human virtue that despises genuine biblical humility because biblical humility acknowledges moral indebtedness to God and is rooted in God awareness: confidence toward God.

The New Testament uses the word in a uniquely Christian context. No Greek writer before the Christian era used it. The correct biblical definition is a deep sense of moral littleness before God. New Testament humility is not about largeness of soul; it is about littleness of soul before God.

The ultimate act of biblical humility is *confident faith*. It is abandonment of confidence in self and utter confidence in God and His promises. Failure to trust God, act on His promises, step out on His Word, or exercise His graces and gifts because of an inferiority complex, insecurity, fear, timidity, or some other psychological maladjustment *is not biblical humility*. There are few things more offensive than phony Christian humility generated by the legalist.

Humility has nothing to do with external diffidence, mildness of speech, or a lack of personal psychological wholeness. A lot of psychological dysfunction masquerades in the church as humility. J. Konrad Hölè has a poignant insight into church dysfunction: "The only thing worse than not recognizing something that is dysfunctional is thinking you need more of it to produce change."[11]

If our definition of humility is erroneous, more of this so-called humility will not help us individually or the Church corporately. The timid, the insecure, and the fearful have a special reservation in hell along with a select company of offenders (see Rev. 21:8). They will always view the faithful, the bold, and the confident as proud and arrogant and will accuse them of lacking humility.

MEEKNESS

(*Gr.* Praútes)

When considering meekness it is hard to avoid the effeminate stereotypical image portrayed in religious art and elsewhere. Aristotle defined meekness as the state between utter irascibility and lacking gall. Imagine an "emotion scale" with anger for no reason on the left, and never getting angry for any reason on the right. Biblical meekness would be the middle point on the scale of emotion. Meekness is getting angry for the right reason, at the right time, in the right way.[12] This definition makes the following incidents (and others like them) in our Lord's life a demonstration of meekness, perfectly consistent with Greek thought and God's character. They are acts of *meekness*:

- Driving out the moneychangers (John 2)

- Calling Peter *satan*, to his face (Matt. 16:23)

- Insulting the Judeans by saying they were lying murderers like their father the devil (John 8:44)

- Calling the Judeans names (illegitimate offspring of snakes)[13]

- Disappointing the rich young ruler (Mark 10)

We rarely think of meekness as the presence of passion or emotion, let alone anger. Individuals raised in an atmosphere where expression of legitimate emotion was forbidden, do not realize how deeply conditioned they are and how their interpretation of Scripture has been affected by their upbringing. For them meekness is the *absence* of emotion, a passion-less, passive, external gentility—the "shut up and put up treatment" (often illegitimately projected on women in the husband and wife relationship). This is *not biblical* meekness.

GENTLENESS

(*Gr.* epieíkeia)

Gentleness is frequently interpreted in terms of personality, tem-perament, degree of quietness, external demeanor, or habits of speech. In fact, the external demeanor that many would interpret as gentleness is often a religious façade for cowardice and fear. Some appear gentle because of inability to, or fear of, dealing with issues and people! Some only appear gentle because they have not been provoked in public!

The Greek term is best rendered as "sweet reasonableness." Gentleness recognizes the impossibility of cleaving to all formal law. It anticipates and provides for all cases that emerge and present themselves for a decision. It recognizes the potential damage that can be done in the assertion of legal rights (justice) lest they should be pushed to moral wrongs. It does not urge its own rights to the uttermost, but denies them in part or in full to rectify the injustice of justice. It is a moderating grace.

This definition brings gentleness out of the realm of personality, style, and feeling. It is the quality that is frequently *lacking* in Christians—especially legalists. Legalists demand exacting justice and conformity to the letter of the law, untempered by mercy or consideration of the weakness of the offender. I have seen many individuals who appear sweet and gentle in their temperament, but when provoked, wronged, or violated, manifest the cruelest, demanding, legalistic spirit imaginable. This is *not biblical* gentleness.

Understanding these terms biblically rather than from our culture helps us understand the legitimacy of the passion Paul used in his response to the Galatians. Legalism is not a fringe or marginal issue in the Church. Paul recognized it for what it was, understood the criticality of a corrupted seed, and responded with appropriate emotion.

Where are the Asiatic and Palestinian churches today? Gone. Even apostolic heritage does not guarantee our future if we allow the corrupt seed of legalism to root and blossom in our hearts or churches.

End Notes:

1. In Genesis 2:18, Eve is described as a "help meet" or help mate, which could also be defined as "a strengthening partner, completely suitable for, a perfect fit, rightly adaptable to."

2. This book is not a technical work, but an interested reader can find more information in any of the available commentaries concerning North and South Galatia theories.

3. Gnosticism is a philosophy that flouts all moral restraint, moral authority, or moral convention, and promotes living a dissolute life.

4. This explanation is admittedly superficial and simplified for contextual continuity. Gnosticism was addressed by the apostle John in his Gospel and all his Epistles, and by Paul primarily in Ephesians and Colossians. Peter also addresses it in his Epistles, but less systematically than Paul or John.

5. In Paul's day, there were very strict cultural proprieties concerning letter writing. To omit an opening salutation was an insult and let the reader know from the start that what was to follow was not going to be very pleasant.

6. John Eldredge, *Wild at Heart: Discovering the Secret of a Man's Soul* (Nashville: Thomas Nelson, 2001), p. 22.

7. Eldredge, *Wild at Heart*, p. 19.

8. Leon J. Podles, *The Church Impotent: the Feminization of Christianity* (Dallas: Spence Publishing, 1999), pp. 17, 33.

9. The strategy of American revivalists in the Second Great Awakening in the 1830's was to approach men through their wives. Women were converted first and then they exerted more or less successful pressure upon fathers, brothers, husbands, and sons to join them in the church (Podles, *The Church Impotent*, p. 3). Throughout the nineteenth century women outnumbered men two to one in church, which matched the ratio in the Great Awakening (Podles, *The Church Impotent*, p. 17). During the First Great Awakening most converts were young (aged 15-25), without children, and predominantly female (Barbara L. Epstein, *Politics of Domesticity: Women, Evangelism and Temperance in Nineteenth Century America* [Middletown, Conn.: Wesleyan University Press, 1981], p. 47; cited by Podles, *The Church Impotent*, p. 18.

10. For instance: music styles in the Church—Spurgeon called his music department the *War Room!*

11. J. Konrad Hölé, *You Were Born a Champion; Don't Die a Loser* (Minneapolis: World Press, 1999), p. 37.

12. This is not biblical justification for expressions of carnality pretending to be righteous.

13. In Matthew 12:34 and 23:33, Jesus uses the terms "generation of vipers" and "brood of vipers." The ancients believed that snakes reproduced asexually—without fathers. Jesus was insulting the Judean claim to lineage with Abraham. He called them illegitimate snake children.

Sell It with "Lex" Appeal[1]

As Christians, we are often quick to point out the performance-oriented foundations and tendencies of non-Christian religions. Individuals outside of Christ worship from the unregenerate Adamic nature that loves to perform in an attempt to find acceptance with God. This should not surprise us. The question is, why do the redeemed frequently live out of the same mentality? How could a church that was established by the apostle Paul himself succumb so readily to the inroads of legalism?

Like Luke Skywalker, we understand the importance of resisting the evil emperor. But, lifting Darth Vader's helmet and discovering he is your father—that's the surprise. Finding the enemy's seed in the Church is a bit disconcerting.

Legalism in the Church is an earthly reflection of the battle in the cosmos. Who has the right to rule? Whose hand is at the helm? Control is a false form of authority and government. Satan cannot have legitimate rulership. Jesus *is* Lord. God's anointed has already been enthroned on Mount Zion.[2]

But satan can, and frequently does, gain illegitimate control on earth. Like Velcro—a fastening system made up of small hooks and loops—legalism is a spirit that appeals to the Adamic nature. The hook side of Velcro is useless without the loop side. Likewise, the hook of the satanic agenda requires a loop in the Adamic nature to effectively work legalism into the Lord's Church. Legalism is attractive. It has *lex* appeal.

IF IT AIN'T BROKE, DON'T FIX IT

If a devious strategy is patently obvious or offensive, it is not effective as deception. It must have appeal. Legalism has been successful since

A.D. 49. From a strategy point of view, that kind of performance would get you in the satanic hall of fame on the first ballot. *Effective deception must be deceiving!* Promoting a bad counterfeit is like trying to sell brown shoes in a tuxedo shop. You can spot a pair a mile away and there ain't no market for 'em.

By definition, deceived persons do not know they are deceived. I have pastorally counseled numerous individuals struggling with various issues. However, I have never had a counseling situation start with, "Pastor, I am so deceived. Would you please help me?" Hardly! A counseling session may *end* with recognition of deception, but it rarely *starts* with one. Legalism is effective because it is unrecognized poison. Like D-Con (a poison for rodents), it tastes good to the ratty old nature but is, in fact, very dangerous.

The Galatians did not wake one morning with a surprise case of spiritual apostasy—infected with some unseen virus. They had witnessed not only conversions, but also miracles in their midst (see Gal. 3:5), yet they took to legalism like trout to PowerBait. The Jerusalem contingent's persuasive presentation lured the Galatians away from manifested Spirit reality and the Person and work of Christ. Why did the Galatians, who had "begun in the Spirit" (Gal. 3:3), so readily take the bait of an alternate reality? What made them bite?

There are at least six ways that performance-based religion appealed to the Galatians and continues to appeal to believers in every generation. They are:

1. The Appeal of Culture
2. The Appeal of Apparent Authority
3. The Appeal of Identity
4. The Appeal of Scrupulousness
5. The Appeal of Superiority
6. The Influence of Supernatural Occult Power

THE APPEAL OF CULTURE

The inhabitants of Galatia were a passionate race, culturally prone to fickleness.[3] The Judaizers could not accept that Gentiles were coming into the privilege of covenantal relationship with *their* God, free of Judaic laws and practices. In the mind of the Judaizers, salvation belonged to them. They were the custodians of Torah, the Covenant, and the God-sanctioned administrators of what was holy and what was not. Circumcision did not just identify Israel as the covenant people, but it distinguished them ethnically and culturally as well. The tendency to conform our image of God and His expectations for us (and others) to the image of our culture is imperceptibly strong. It is also the root of idolatry and the appeal of legalism.

American, White, Anglo-Saxon, Protestant culture can masquerade as the image of Christ. For instance, a quiet and reserved demeanor, personality, or temperament may be esteemed as Christ-like. In many families, it is considered a virtue to never speak the truth if it hurts someone's feelings. Peace is to be maintained at the expense of individual psychological wellness. An individual who is outspoken or interpersonally direct is considered rude or insensitive.

On my father's side of the family, my English/Scotch ancestors arrived on this continent on the second boat to hit Plymouth after the Mayflower. Not expressing one's emotions, saying nothing in the present of an offense, stuffing hurt feelings, etc., were values that permeated my father's cultural ethics and sense of right and wrong behavior. Unfortunately, emotional coolness and reserve is not necessarily a Kingdom virtue. Jesus was not a New England Yankee.

In many Latin or Mediterranean cultures, people are quite likely to express themselves with a great deal of emotional intensity, which is soon forgotten. (My mother's side of the family is Latin/Gallic, which might explain my neurosis!) Emotional reserve is viewed as insincerity and a lack of genuineness. Which is "Christ-like?" New England reserve or Mediterranean passion? Which is biblical? Neither and both! The Gospel of Christ transcends culture at the same time it redeems and sanctifies it. We must learn to separate culture, preference, and tradition from a biblical Kingdom ethos lest we be found, like the Galatians, to be departing from Christ because of culture's appeal.

In Galatia, the culture of the Judaizers had the same intimidating effect as historical European culture or American culture today. The Gentiles, recent converts from paganism, had no history or background with Yahweh, His covenants, and His precepts. Then one day, a group of Jerusalem brethren walk in, fully dressed in their ethnic and rabbinical garments, perhaps carrying a Torah scroll or some other scrolls under their arms. The appeal of the culture would be psychologically overwhelming and, as such, was a tremendous influence allowing their legalistic doctrine to begin to take root in the hearts of the Galatians.

In today's world, America is the dominant culture. It is incredibly effective in exporting itself, mostly through its mercantile strength. Unfortunately, it seems we export the absolutely worst elements of our culture the most effectively. Other countries become the spiritual land-fills for toxic American cultural waste. Developing countries seem to gravitate to our money and the cultural sewage that accompanies it, rather than our virtues. When a dominant culture (rather than Kingdom revelation) is enforced in the Church, a form of legalism has taken root that is a hairsbreadth away from racism.

THE APPEAL OF APPARENT AUTHORITY

Like the president of the United States dropping in on Beaver Holler, Kentucky, the Judaizers carried some authoritative clout in Galatia. They were from the biggest and best church in the region, The First Church of Jerusalem, Inc., led by none other than "The Rock" himself—Christ's hand-picked leader. They had a 4,000-year legacy with God. The theologically educated keepers of Torah (God's Word) were literate, passionate, and sincere. Who would not be impressed? Their credentials gave their doctrine a high status in the hearts of the Galatian believers. Legalism rode into main-street Galatia on a finely outfitted white stallion of apparent authority—but the rider had a black hat.

How do we know that the appeal of authority was at work in Galatia? Paul spent the first chapter and a half of his letter to the Galatians *vindicating his credentials*, his call, and his authority. The credentials Paul bore were not the endorsements of ecclesiastical council, but the revelation of Jesus Christ, the marks in his body, and the character of Christ (see Gal. 1:1; 11-17).

Legalism is often brought into the church by means of impressive biblical authority, charm, persuasive personality, and giftedness. Those with history and experience in God can unconsciously intimidate the young and the inexperienced. A lie, untruth, or subjective opinion—if repeated enough with conviction, authority, and passion—has the power to shape people's lives. Every two-bit tyrant and dictator in history has known this and used it with great effectiveness.

I was once in an environment where the head of the organization was what I might generously call a Christian mystic—heavily inclined toward dreams, visions, subjective impressions, and experiences. Unfortunately, the individual was also head of a Bible school. He frequently taught doctrine from his dreams and visions—a formula for disaster.[4] Because the gentleman was a highly gifted and respected senior man, generations of young and impressionable people filled their notebooks with his teachings, not realizing that the biblical and exegetical base was faulty at best and, at worst, groundless—and even, in some specific instances, cultic.

The more potent our personality and the stronger our base of biblical "facts," the more vital it is that our message, life, and ministry be "on track." We must judge a message or doctrine on its substance, not on the apparent authority of the one presenting it or the persuasiveness of the presentation. Failure to do so becomes the foundation for unrecognized legalism.

TOXIC AUTHORITY

It is easy to criticize leaders. It does not take a brain surgeon or Philadelphia lawyer to find fault. Contrary to the imaginations of some independent, unsubmissive, and ungovernable saints, finding fault with leaders is not the spiritual gift of discernment. The issue is not the blind and unquestioning obedience expected in a cult, but how one questions spiritual authority in an honoring way. *In a legal and controlling atmosphere, any question, even if presented honorably, is viewed as disloyalty* or deviation from the local vision. The individual with the question is afterward looked at with suspicion as "not really being *with* us."

I was once in a church environment where the leadership told individual members whom they could marry, where they could work, where they should live, whether or not they should have children, how many children they could have, and so on. The corrupt spiritual authority that the leadership possessed gave their deviant doctrines great weight among the new converts of my generation—we did not know any better.

Playing on legitimate principles of subordinate loyalty to authority, corrupt leaders exert leverage to obtain compliance with aberrant doctrines. The Judaizers used the same leverage in Galatia.

For some reason, professional Christian ministry attracts the psychologically dysfunctional and terminally insecure like flies to rotten meat. Deeply damaged individuals are often drawn to the public esteem that a pulpit minister may receive. Looking for personal validation in the pulpit is like expecting a Novocain-free tooth extraction to feel good.

Insecure ministers and critical subordinates make a toxic local church brew. Secure fathers and loyal sons should be able to have strong disagreements without experiencing relational breach. However, fear and control are frequently misused and abused by those in authority to keep honest inquiry at bay. Insecure ministers use their position of authority to avoid legitimate requests for explanation and clarification. Psychologically healthy fathers expect their sons to not only honorably challenge them, but also to surpass them in experience of Christ.

The prevailing orthodoxy of one generation often uses the appeal of authority to resist innovation or adjustment to the corrupt or incorrect practices within its own generation. Those who possess authority are often reluctant to give it up. Frequently the next generation has to "leave" in order to find their place. For instance, the Roman Catholic Church resisted the Protestant Reformers. The Protestant Reformers resisted the Methodist Revivalists. The Methodist brothers resisted the Pentecostal renewal and so on. Multi-generational and trans-generational vision and methodology are key to avoiding this dynamic within a local church or organization.

The appeal of authority is a powerful means by which legalism and aberrant doctrines of many kinds subtly work into the Church. The remedy is to major on majors—the sound exposition and presentation of the Person and work of Christ, His cross, believed in and applied—and to stay away from marginal pet doctrines of gifted and persuasive people.

THE APPEAL OF IDENTITY

Urban youth workers know that the desire to "belong" is a power-ful force of human psychology—far-reaching in societal impact. Our streets are littered with angry young men in gangs. Indoctrinated by the public schools with the nihilistic philosophy of macroevolution,[5] young people live every meaningless day of their lives in a society character-ized by fatherlessness, relational abandonment, isolation, materialism, and family breakdown.

Young people *will find* their place of "belongingness"—one way or the other. If not from healthy sources (adults, family, church, civic organ-izations, etc.), then they will find it on the street. Although distorted, a gang provides a sense of purpose, place, structure, authority (even a gang has a leader) and cause—more than our schools and society offer. Even if personal treatment becomes abusive, the gang member will gladly endure it rather than lose his or her sense of identity with the group.

Similarly, a believer will often endure a toxic church environment because, though poisonous unto death, it provides a place of identity and human relationship. The spiritual substance of the life of Christ is regularly sacrificed by the Church on the altar of humanity's primal need for identity.

It's As Easy As One, Two, Three

In order for any group of people to achieve a large goal, only three simple ingredients are necessary:

1. Identity

2. Training

3. A Cause

Eleven men in a locker room do not make a football team. However, if you provide uniforms (team identity), train them, and inspire them to a greater cause, they will achieve more as a unified team than what their collective individualities could attain. Give a boy a uniform, flag, slogan, and a cause, and you have reached not only today's boy, but made tomorrow's man—for better or worse. Lord Baden-Powell understood this when he founded the Boy Scouts. Our military operates by it. Hitler used it for the Hitler Youth, and Lenin used it with the Red Youth. Trained individuals awakened to a cause are a mob. Trained individuals who share a common identity are an army. An army can easily scatter a mob.

Satan is content to let believers in a local church be a collection of trained individuals working for the Lord's cause or the local church's vision. What he will resist is discovery of the essential and primary ingredient of their individual and corporate success—their identity. Successful Kingdom advance begins by recognizing, believing in, and acting upon our identity in Christ. If satan can obscure the believer's identity, or cause the believer to embrace false religious alternates to his or her identity, the church will just be a mob, not a conquering army. Satan's army of demonic hosts has easily scattered the well-trained church-mob. Without identity, the cause is lost. Trying harder and working more will not compensate for failure in identity.

IDENTITY THEFT

Nehemiah 13:7-9 demonstrates this principle in typological form. Eliashib, the corrupt high priest, prepared a chamber in the temple for Tobiah the Ammonite—an act forbidden by God (see Deut. 23:3).

An Ammonite did not have the *correct covenant identity* to be residing in the house of God. Yet, once allowed in the temple, Tobiah took it as his own, displacing all the items belonging to the Lord and bringing in his own. He took a place in the temple he was not entitled to and made it his. Next, he forced the Levites, the singers, and the servants of the Lord to forsake their God-ordained identity, calling, and ministry to go back to the fields to *work*. Rather than living from the Lord's provision for them (the tithe and offering), they were forced to earn their living as field laborers—functioning outside of their God-ordained identity and calling. Because they were outside of their place and identity, they were cut off from their birthright inheritance. Nehemiah's response in Jerusalem was as passionate as Paul's in Galatia: Throw the stuff out of the house (see Neh. 13:8)!

This is a picture of what happens when a corrupt, legal, religious influence is brought into the Church: God's anointed covenant sons and daughters lose their identity and are forced to work at *producing* Kingdom life rather than *freely partaking* of the King's life. There is confusion of identity and function. Sons become slaves. Privilege is lost. Rather than living from the riches of the believer's inheritance in Christ, the performance-based religionist works to earn his identity, strives to produce his or her calling.

THE APPEAL OF SCRUPULOUSNESS

Some of the well-known mass-market retailers often conduct coloring contests for children in support of charities. A standardized picture is given to entrants, categorized by age, who then color the picture and resubmit it for scoring. The children who do the best job of staying within the lines win the prize. This is fine marketing and promotional strategy but it is lousy Christian theology and practice. Many believers' personal experience with God is like a coloring contest: God has given us the outline picture—the Bible. It delineates all His expectations—determines the lines I must stay within. If I just do my best to stay within God's lines, to try *really* hard, to color *really* well, maybe the great Judge will score me a winner and I will be rewarded both now and in the hereafter.

Our entire culture is set up that way. It is in the fabric of our soul. From the time of our first day of school until we retire, we are rewarded for good behavior and punished for bad. Performing well gets us ahead in every arena: family, school, job, or unfortunately, the church. A poor performance means you lose the race, the show gets canceled, the job is lost. It is all up to you. In the midst of this climate, we experience the refreshing breezes of the new birth in Christ.

In the beginning of our faith, we may understand theologically that we are justified by faith, but after conversion it is common to spend the bulk of our life living as if the rest of Christianity is about how good a colorer I can be. His Kingdom does not go forward based on performance and scoring. It advances by death and resurrection. His expectations for proper behavior have never changed; the source of life in the believer has. I am not called to live scrupulously, but abundantly.

The Judaizers were extremely sincere and religiously scrupulous folks. They were not "bad people." They were just wrong people. Their message to the Galatians was not—"*depart from* the living God, turn and serve other gods." Rather, their teaching required that the Galatians could and *should* get closer to God by doing more to please Him than Christ had already accomplished on their behalf. They appealed to the Galatians to live more scrupulously for God by adhering to the Mosaic law in order to earn the right to claim the status of sons and daughters of God.

Satan's strategy is not irreligion. His strategy of deception since the Garden has been to make humanity as good and religious as possible apart from Christ and His cross. His strategy is to relationally alienate the children from the Father through works and legal religion. The essence of legal religion is meeting God's expectations for moral behavior while at the same time being relationally alienated from Him.

The Judaizers took advantage of the Galatians legitimate desire to walk pleasing before God and turned it against God's Christ. They did not understand the breadth and the scope of the change ushered in by Christ—not a change in the requirements of moral behavior, but a change in relationship and life source. They were being scrupulous about details of which God had forever changed. From a "present-truth" perspective, it is always dangerous to scrupulously measure what is presently endorsed of God by what *used to be* endorsed by God. Although Christ crucified is the eternal standard, we must be willing to change emphasis with the Holy

Spirit. Legal Christian religion is the enemy of the Gospel and it always looks right.

CAREFUL TO A FAULT

It is very easy for any pulpit minister to point out people's deficiencies and preach at them to improve. Who in a crowd cannot do better in some area of their life? It takes no grace or anointing to preach to people's deficiencies. Such sermons take advantage of sincere individual's desires to please God. Ministers who emphasize the call to responsible living before grounding believers in their change of identity fail to understand that, in Christ, God has already been pleased. They are also unconsciously defeating the very purpose they hope to accomplish. Shouting at a fish to stop swimming is ridiculous. It is in the fish's nature to be in the water. However, if a squirrel spends all his time in the pool, the issue becomes awakening him to his true identity, not exhorting him to get out of the pool!

My scrupulousness does not bring me closer to God. Careful living cannot produce a son. But a son can live carefully. For example, I am my mother's son. There is nothing I can do to make myself more her son or less her son. My status is determined by birth. I can bring shame or honor to her, but I cannot be more "sonly" by my behavior. I can live out of my sonship, or I can live out of external code.

Legalists forget what humanity's condition is. Humanity's problem is not wrong behavior. Wrong behavior can be corrected by right behavior—scrupulous and careful living. Humanity's problem is a wrong condition and a broken relationship. This is the offense of the cross and the offense of Christianity. Our message to humanity is: "You cannot fix your condition by your behavior. You are wrong as a state of being." Because of our condition, we need someone else to save us. Individuals often start their Christian walk with a semblance of this understanding, but shortly after they experience church life, they begin to act like their careful and scrupulous living somehow makes them more pleasing to God—that they can get closer to Him by reason of their carefulness.

In Christ, we are as close to God as we are ever going to get. We cannot get closer by worship, singing, or careful living. We have already been brought near by the work of Another. We can do nothing to change our relationship to the Father. What we *can* do is yield to His life by embracing His cross, and then manifest His life by the Holy Spirit through us in any number of legitimate manifestations. I am not endorsing a casual or careless Christianity. The issue is one of source. Is the source of our obedience our determinate will and effort to live to please God, or is it the life of the Son of God in us freely given and freely yielded to?

ACHIEVE TO RECEIVE

The problem with an emphasis on scrupulous living is that it appeals to the unregenerate Adamic nature. The unregenerate nature loves to achieve. It loves to have the requirement explicitly stated so that it can exercise itself to meet the requirement. Since the Adamic nature is religiously legal, scrupulousness produces legalism in a church. Many of the individuals in the cults put Christians to shame with their scrupulous behavior. If careful and scrupulous living proves I am a Christian, what are we to do with the following chart comparing typical behavioral qualities of a well-known cult[6] member in the West and a supposed born-again Christian:

Quality or Virtue	Cult Member	Christian
Doesn't use profanity	X	X
Doesn't abuse substances	X	X
Provides for the family	X	X
Helps others	X	X
Reads the Bible	X	X
Prays regularly	X	X
Attends their fellowship regularly	X	X
Gives financially	X	X
Loves their children	X	X
Loves their mate	X	X
Serves others	X	X

As you can see, careful living does not make someone a Christian. Regeneration by the Holy Spirit does. It is entirely possible to meet all the requirements of the Bible and be completely out of fellowship with God via the Holy Spirit. My clean living does not prove I am born again or that I am a son of God. What then is the proof of our Christian genuineness if it is not our behavior? Paul makes it clear in Galatians. There is one thing that Adam cannot copy, that human nature cannot emulate: the reality of the indwelling Holy Spirit and the concrete manifestations of His presence.

My personal theological background was one that attempted to emphasize issues of holiness. The first 13 years of my experience were spent navel gazing. Looking inward and trying to discover faults and blemishes in my character. If I discovered one (and there were plenty), it then became the source of mental and emotional preoccupation. I would literally spend hours, praying and at times fasting, asking God to forgive me and to make me more like Him, hoping that by my careful living, I would finally be acceptable to Him. Surprisingly perhaps to some, I really did not make too much progress in overcoming any of the weaknesses of character over which I was obsessing. I certainly was miserable, despairing, and an obnoxious hyper-religious pain in the keister to everyone around me...what a great testimony!

Consider this: As a parent, how would you feel if every interaction with your child was taken up with the child pointing out every fault he or she possessed, carrying on about it, and begging you for love, acceptance, and forgiveness? I trust this is self-evidently absurd. Yet how many thousands of Christians live this way in their relationship to God? Unsure of acceptance, their status before God hinges on the thoroughness of the last sin exam they may have done. We attribute less psychological normalcy to our Heavenly Father than we do our earthly parents!

Over a process of time, re-education, training, and divine encounter, I came to realize that God liked me—that through no work of my own, He made me His son. Because I am His son, I have a new life source. I am not responsible to inspect myself for blemish. I am responsible to relate to Him; and together, in a real and genuine relationship, we engage in a life process that results in character change. At any given moment in time, I am only responsible for what my Father talks to me about (reveals to me from the Scripture) at that moment. I am not being scored on how well I am staying within the lines in the contest of life. He has planted me in life and I have already won the contest. It is not necessary for me to present the laundry list of my personal failures to him 24-7. He already knows anyway. My responsibility as a believer is to exchange love and life, and from this exchange, holiness results.

This painfully simple, basic, and foundational truth revolutionized my life. "The strength of sin is the law" (1 Cor. 15:56). By focusing on sin, I do not defeat it—I energize it. Preaching hard on a specific sin is usually not a sign of holiness. It is usually a sign that the very sin preached against is manifest in some shape or form in the life of the one preaching it. The problem with a lot of holiness preaching is that it is counterproductive. It actually promotes self-awareness and self-centeredness rather than Christ-awareness and Christ-consciousness.

THE FAMILY NAME

What then is the key to responsible Christian behavior if not carefulness and scrupulousness? It is the family name. Often when children are small, they appeal to their parents to do something that other children in the neighborhood are doing. For whatever reason, the parents do not want their children to participate. The child's query is, "Why? Johnny down the street gets to do it! Why can't I?" The parental response is usually, "That may be all right for Johnny, but Johnny is not my son. You are. We do not do that in our family." Not only does this parental response serve to mold a child's behavior and values, it reinforces in them a sense of place and belonging. It is a matter of a difference in deposit. Instead of depositing the "don't do it rule" in the soul of the child, you have deposited family identity. You have given them identity, not code.

It is the same in our Christian walk. We do not obey because of the law; we obey because we bear a family image. We have been regenerated with a new seed—literally "re-gened" according to the DNA of our Heavenly Father. Sonship produces responsible behavior, but responsible behavior can never produce a son. The source of responsible Christian behavior is the revelation of our identity.

Legalism and the living out of one's convictions and scruples, rather than the revelation and realization of resurrection life, will always produce a distortion of Kingdom life and Christianity. Just as Paul said that being under the law was a sign of childishness, the most externally scrupulous Christian is not always the most mature. They might be the most infantile. Scrupulous Christian living is a delusional malady, yet it appeals to many because "If I can make my vessel shine better than my neighbor's, I will be superior to him."

THE APPEAL OF SUPERIORITY

The Judaizers appealed to the universal human desire to set oneself above others. By demanding of the Galatians external observances, they were saying: "If you do these things, then you will be just a notch above the rest of the believers in the world. This grace thing is ok, but if you *really* want to be spiritual, like *we are*, you *must* do these things." Legal religion always appeals to the pride of possessing superior knowledge, self-achievement, self-vindication, and self-justification. Legal Christian religionists will always be hard on others because deep down they really believe they are better than others through their own efforts: efforts of holiness, study, or charismatic manifestations.

If I can obey nine of God's requirements, and you can only keep seven, I am more advanced, more spiritual than you are and I can use my advanced standing to dominate or control you. A legalist believes that by their superior performance that they somehow have leverage with God and over others.

Oftentimes the greatest blessings of God, insights into the Word or revelation, unfortunately do not result in humility and thankfulness, but a spirit of elitism and isolation. I have experienced this firsthand. At one time in my Christian experience, I belonged to a group who believed they had more superior biblical revelation than others. Indeed, in many ways, the group was blessed with great "deeper life" insights into the Word of God. However, the group was extremely sectarian, isolationist, and superior. In fact, they believed they were so superior that they were above the task of evangelizing. They believed that our group was the man-child of Revelation 12, or Holy of Holy groups, and our calling was higher than other believers. We were called to minister unto God (see Ezek. 44; the Zadok priesthood).

Soul-winning was something that "outer court" Christians were assigned to. I can remember being specifically taught, "The Baptists can save them. We are called to mature them. We will take them into the deeper things." We were taught that evangelism is "OK," but that when the glory of God is really on the Church (of course, that was "us"), the Gentiles will come to the light of our rising. Therefore, it is somewhat a waste of time and energy to be highly evangelistic—it will all happen sovereignly and somewhat effortlessly when our little church shines with the glory of God.

The arrogance and offensiveness of such a statement should be self-evident. It betrays a spirit of superiority. I was so young in the Lord and naïve at the time that I sincerely believed that if the other churches in town would just agree with us that revival would break out! I was honestly shocked that other churches did not see it that way. I marveled at their blindness! Oy—who was the blind one! (P.S. Our church never grew too much…fancy that.)

ASSIGNMENT ALIGNMENT

Sometimes the vision, unique task, or Kingdom emphasis that God assigns a local congregation becomes the root of legalism and superiority. The unique assignment becomes a basis of boasting or comparing one's fellowship to another. Of course, each group believes what God has given them is the latest, the "cutting edge." Others who are not equally assigned are viewed as being "not quite with it." An elitist spirit of superiority creeps in. I have personally seen this dynamic repeated multiple times among good people.

Let's consider just a couple of divine assignments as examples: family and destiny.

Family. Some local churches have a strong emphasis on family and education. There is surely nothing wrong with that. However, if one is not careful, worship is directed at the altar of family, marriage, children, and home schooling, not the Person of Jesus Christ. The reason folks gather is no longer unto the Lord in His Person. It is worship at a foreign altar in the name of Christ. In those spiritual climates, should a family opt to put their children in public school (as an example), they are ostracized as not having "the vision." Of course, family is a *crucial* matter! But Paul did not preach a "family message." He preached Christ and Him crucified. You can scan the entire Book of Acts and not find a single sermon on the importance of family. Approximately 30 years' record of apostolic preaching and nothing on the family. (P.S. The love of God is never mentioned in Acts either. Makes one wonder why we emphasize what we do…but that is another book!)

Destiny. The downside of a strong destiny message is that it can have a subtle appeal to self-advancement. Destiny messages usually emphasize *my* future, what a great person *I* will be, what great things God will do through *me*, how *I* will change the world, and so on. That is fine. But if destiny is preached apart from the Person and cross of Christ, it will become the seedbed of an unrecognized legal spirit that appeals to the Adamic nature's desire to achieve and self-advance. If self-advancement does not occur quite as fast as one would desire or expect, discouragement, disillusionment, bitterness, and resentment will creep into the heart of the one who has embraced a destiny message over a cross message.

Our divine assignment can subtly become the object of our worship rather than God Himself. There are any number of *legitimate lesser emphases* that God may call a church to reflect. But when the lesser thing becomes the greater thing, we have lost our way. Our message has opened the doors for legal spirits that will torment our lives and our churches. Just as the Galatians did not recognize the slippery slope they were heading down, so in our day, vigilance must be exercised to see that Christ is not removed from His place of preeminence within His own house and people. The devil is always well dressed.

THE INFLUENCE OF SUPERNATURAL OCCULT POWER

> *"Oh foolish Galatians, who hath bewitched you"* *(Galatians 3:1).*

After expending considerable energy defending the legitimacy of his call and ministry in the first two chapters of his letter, Paul explodes in an insulting rhetorical outburst in chapter three. He calls the Galatians *fools*. In our culture, to be called a fool is not exactly a compliment, but somewhat of a mild insult—if there is such a thing. To us, the word *fool* can have the connotation of a benign buffoon, a harmless, happy-go-lucky fellow who does not know any better. The Greek word means to be completely lacking intelligence. Perhaps a modern English equivalent would be: Idiots! Not exactly a seeker sensitive approach to ministry! After that heart-warming and endearing phrase, he then proceeds to tell them that they are not only idiots, but also the blind victims of occult powers.

Bewitched literally means "to come under the spell of the evil eye." For Semites or Mediterranean people, light and darkness were believed to be physical substance. The eye was thought to project either. For instance, the eyes of the blind were not viewed as incapable of receiving light, as we would think, but considered to actually emanate darkness.[7] The writers of the Poetical books refer to the eye as reflecting the condition of the soul: consumed with grief, dim with sorrow, abounding with bounty, etc. (see Job 17:7; Ps. 31:9; 88:9; Prov. 22:9). The eye was linked like a pipe or channel to the soul. Therefore, in their minds, what was in the soul could come out of the eye. This was not just a quaint metaphor. Good or evil "soul-stuff" was believed to emanate from the eye. In one of his poems, Theocritus (Greek) used a word (*báskanos*) meaning to destroy with the eyes. To cast the evil eye brought demonic powers out of the soul and projected them on another person.

Over time, the word developed the nuance of meaning to mislead by pretenses as if by magic arts, to fascinate, or to influence by a charm. It is hard for modern Westerners to understand how deeply set this belief system was among the ancients. The belief in the evil eye remains to this day in parts of the Mediterranean, Mid East, and among those who descend from those regions of the world.

The spiritual energy of legalism is demonic. In Second Thessalonians 2:1-10, Paul speaks of a great last day deception, a move by the man of sin (the son of perdition, the antichrist) to oppose God, exalt himself, and sit in the temple showing himself as God. A large segment of American Evangelicalism believes this activity will occur in a literal rebuilt temple, in literal Jerusalem. Perhaps, but it seems untenable to me. Let Paul interpret Paul.

Throughout the New Testament, Paul makes it *plainly* and *emphatically* clear: The believer, more specifically the corporate Church, is the temple of God (see 1 Cor. 3:16; 6:19). God no longer abides in buildings. It is contrary to the rest of Paul's doctrine to believe that he is talking about a literal building and a piece of real estate in Palestine. Just as Tobiah took his place where he did not belong and drove out the covenant sons and heirs, the place where the antichrist will try to move in and take his seat is in the heart of the believer—the true seat of God's government on earth. That is where the most corrupting and damaging influence can occur. As satan's corrupting influence was first manifested in the very courts of heaven, in the Garden, and in Galatia, so it will be in the end: The corrupting rebellion will *be in the house*, the New Covenant temple of God, the Church.

The antichrist's last day strategy is to accomplish with the allure of performance-based religion what he could not accomplish through the centuries by persecution: corrupt and destroy God's true temple, the Church, by Christ-less religion in the name of Christ. Appealing legalistic religion and other lesser distractions, which oppose and exalt themselves against the preeminence of Christ, will attempt to move believers away from pure love, devotion, and service to Him, His Church, and the world. The love of many will wax cold.

CHAPTER THREE

End Notes

1. *Lex* is Latin for "law."

2. In Psalm 2, the Lord laughs at the nations in rebellion because the Messiah has already been set, anointed, and invested on Mount Zion with the office of ruler.

3. The interested reader is referred to the many commentaries that describe Galatian culture.

4. Teaching doctrine from dreams and visions is the subjective curse of the charismatic branch of the Church.

5. Nihilism: a philosophy that life is meaningless, senseless, and useless; there is no objective ground of truth, especially moral truth. Since evolution teaches that we came from nothing and are going nowhere, that our existence is due to the chance collision of microscopic particles, it is fundamentally a nihilistic philosophy.

6. For instance, consider Mormonism or Jehovah's Witnesses.

7. The interested reader is referred to: Bruce J. Malina and Richard L. Rohrbaugh, *Social Science Commentary on the Synoptics* (Minneapolis: Fortress, 1992), and *Social Science Commentary of the Gospel of John* (Minneapolis: Fortress, 1998).

CHAPTER FOUR

"Doc, What's Ailing Me?"

I once read a survey that listed "medical misdiagnosis and malpractice" as the fourth leading cause of death in America. Scary. Hospitals can be dangerous to your health! Although my extended family has enjoyed the blessing of relatively good health (which we do not take for granted), we have come close to being part of that statistic. At times we have felt like patients in Los Arms Hospital at the mercy of Dr. Howard, Dr. Fine, and Dr. Howard (aka Moe, Larry, and Curly).[1] Although I am thankful to be alive in the 21st century's version of medicine rather than the 15th century's, my faith is in God. After all, doctors are still "practicing" medicine.

What's the point of this cheery personal digression? *Misdiagnosis can be lethal*. If the disease does not kill you, misdiagnosis or malpractice will. If I was unaware that I had a disease because of misdiagnosis, I would be quite dispassionate about whether or not I obtained the cure. *Passion for the cure is determined by awareness of need*. We must recognize our need to value and apply God's cure.

We understand that the "hook" of legalism appeals to the "loop" of the Adamic nature. However, before considering an appropriate treatment for legalism, we need correct self-diagnosis. How does the virus of legalism manifest itself in human thinking and behavior? Let's examine some symptoms of legalism so we can effectively apply Calvary's all-sufficient resources to bear on them.

INSECURITY

Innumerable Hollywood movie plots are based on an obsessively dysfunctional individual who withdraws into an imaginary world to escape unbearable life circumstances. In the reclusive fantasy world, the individual finds an Edenic inner place of functionality and competence for his or her irrational behavior. The character's real life failures are pushed out of consciousness by irrelevant competence as he or she becomes master in a smaller universe.

Insecurity in a Christian can be a manifestation of legalism for the same reason. When someone's life circumstances or mental world are characterized by uncertainty, the Adamic response is to form a workable life-system in which a person can at least gain a sense of safety, stability, and wellness. By having a rigid set of self-defined God expectations, insecure believers use legalism to reduce the size of their cosmos.

Christianity's (or the Church's) appeal to an outsider can be the misconception that religion brings security in an insecure world. The Church supposedly provides the black and white that is missing in the world that has gone terribly gray. When insecure new converts find not only moral right and wrong in God's Kingdom, but considerable grayness in some areas, they will often choose to embrace binding legal principles over gray vagueness. The new converts replace their uncertain and broken philosophy for a new "Christian" philosophy that is supposed to make things "all better."

Sometimes this dynamic is little more than a change of operator's manuals, but not a change of operators. The murky operator's manual of the world is swapped for God's allegedly crystal-clear manual, the Bible. Unfortunately, rather than finding well-being and security in relationship to a Person (Jesus Christ as revealed by the Holy Spirit, through the Word) the individual's need is met by embracing the false structures of rigid legalism and a view that the Bible has the answer for all of life's problem's[2]

The passion with which individuals may cling to the new operator's manual is a manifestation of a legal infection. We must hold tightly and devotedly to the Person Jesus. We must hold loosely to our understanding of Him. He is unchangeable and my *relationship* to Him is eternal. My *understanding* of Him may be deficient at any given point in time and is subject to growth and change.

ANTINOMY

The Scriptures are full of a linguistic feature called antinomy. An antinomy is a direct contradiction between two statements, laws, or principles that are equally true and both necessary. An example of antinomy is how one should respond to sin in someone else's life. The Scripture says that love covers a multitude of sins (see Prov. 10:12). Therefore, that is how we should respond to a brother who sins, right? Well, maybe. The Scripture also says that "open rebuke is better than secret love," and if you see a brother in sin, rebuke him to his face (Prov. 27:5; Luke 17:3). Which is right? Both and neither. The correct response is the one the Spirit chooses. He is Lord over His own Word.

Like an elastic band, in order to be of any use, the two opposing principles must be present and in tension with one another. Relieve the tension in a rubber band by cutting it, and it ceases to be a rubber band! *Remove either pole of an antinomy or relive the tension and the Word of God loses its purpose and function—holding together the full counsel of God.*[3]

Within a local congregation, people's temperaments and gifts will tend to draw them to one response or the other. An unsanctified and insecure mercy gift, for example, will be threatened by the exercise of severity and judgment, even though it is completely biblical to do so in a right spirit. An unsanctified and insecure prophetic or "black and white" temperament will be threatened by the exercise of mercy as to them it will speak of compromise and vacillation.

God's Kingdom life is not found in the uniform and consistent exercise of either extreme. Like electrical current flowing between two opposite poles of a battery, life only happens when there is dynamic interchange between two opposing poles of His grace. Life flows when the tension is always present: when mercy tempers judgment and judgment puts spine in mercy. Only the Spirit of God through us can administer His own diverse anointings in a given situation. Our dependency is in Him.

The insecure legalist who looks for the one-size-fits-all rulebook approach to the Kingdom is in for a very rough ride. Often those in the vicinity of the legalist go for the ride also, whether they want to or not. It is tragic that for the insecure, the rough ride rarely breaks them down to a genuine encounter with the living God, but their typical response is to find a better rule to cover the one that just let them down in some circumstance.

THE OPERATOR'S MANUAL

Imagine that a blind man buys a Black and Decker lawn mower at a rummage sale. His gardener uses it for a few times and it breaks down.

The gardener discovers that the manual that came with it is incorrect, belonging to a different manufacturer's mower. So the gardener goes to the B and D distributor and gets the correct manual for the blind man's mower and gives it to him. Of course, the blind man cannot fix the mower because he lacks the faculty to read the correct manual and lacks the faculty to fix the mower. However, if the blind man should experience the recovery of his sight, he might be able to fix the mower intuitively without the correct manual, or at least be able to read the manual and have a chance of fixing it.

So it is in the Kingdom. Giving the correct manual to the broken and insecure Adamic nature will not produce God's life and God's spirit. On the other hand, experientially heal the Adamic wound—in effect, give sight—then the manual makes sense. Insecure Adam just wants to exchange manuals, not go to the depth necessary to actually engage the living God at a place of personal brokenness to receive what only He has to give. Obtaining a better systems manual for living, even a divinely inspired one, cannot supplant the healing touch of Jesus.

The genuine life of faith, with its uncertainties and inherently unmanageable adventure, is too intimidating for the psychologically insecure. I recently read a paraphrase of the foundation Scripture of the Reformation: "The just shall live by faith" (Rom. 1:17; Hab. 2:4). The author translated it this way: "The righteous thrive in the midst of unpredictable change."[4] For the insecure, life, including life with God, must be reduced to something that is manageable. Even if the philosophy is binding and limiting, the insecure will choose it over the uncertainty that comes with a life of spiritual liberty and faith. Until they are healed, the insecure do not have the psychological faculty to do otherwise, even if they are toting the Bible under their arms and quoting the Scriptures every Sunday. Legalism begets insecurity and insecurity begets legalism.

LIFE BY PRINCIPLE OR THE PRINCIPLE OF LIFE

Many believers misapply a common phrase. The oft-repeated saying is that God desires to teach His children "precept upon precept, line upon line, here a little and there a little." It is assumed that this is the normal, God-ordained way a believer's life is built. Nothing could be further from the truth. One day, I became curious to look for where the phrase actually occurred and was I shocked at what I found. I think you will be also. The phrase is from Isaiah 28:7-15. I trust the reader will agree that the context of a passage is vital to its interpretation.

In Isaiah 28:7-8 the Scripture describes the state of an apostate leadership in the strongest terms. God refers to His leaders, the priests and the prophets, as drunken and filled with their own vomit and filth—not a pretty or a positive picture.

In verse 9 He then makes a rhetorical statement, contextually referring to the priests. Bewailing their apostate condition, the prophet cries, "To whom then will the word of the Lord be revealed?" He rhetorically answers himself: those who are just weaned from the breast—babies. He then bemoans how their apostate condition has forced Him to talk to them: "precept upon precept...line upon line; here a little and there a little" (Isa. 28:10)! At the very least, the implication is that if we are taught that way then we are in a state of babyhood, if not apostasy! That is hardly something a Christian should emulate or model.

The Lord then goes on to make an amazing declaration explaining the reason for the judgment of having to speak to His people by "precept." He refers to the rest that He had for His people, but they would not come unto Him. God had a relational place of rest in His Person (see Heb. 3–4) that Israel of old opted not to pursue, but instead chose to live through adherence to principles.

In Isaiah 28:13 the prophet repeats himself for emphasis, bemoaning that God has to speak to them "precept upon precept...line upon line; here a little and there a little," and then explains God's purpose in speaking in such a way: so that His children would "go, and fall backward, and be broken, and snared, and taken"! The purpose for preceptual instruction is so we will be exhausted from that type of instruction and return to His Person for rest and relationship! It is designed to cause us to fail. As long as we are successful living by precepts, our confidence will be in the precepts rather than the Person who upholds the precepts. If God is to reclaim His relational rest with us, He must destroy every other false foundation, including intellectual confidence in the precepts of His Word that keep us from a vital living relationship with Himself.

We see the thought again in Exodus 19 and 20, the account of Moses and the children of Israel at Mount Sinai. God told Moses He wanted to talk to the people. He told the people to prepare themselves and not touch the mountain lest they die. Moses goes up the mountain, personally encounters God, and the people hear God's voice. Moses comes back down the mountain unharmed. However, even with Moses in front of them as proof, they confess that if someone hears the voice of God they will die. In lieu of personal relationship and engagement with the voice of God, Israel makes a fatal mistake with generational implication. They said, in essence, "Moses, you go talk to God. Find out for us what He wants, tell us what His precepts are, and we will do all you tell us to do—but we won't speak to Him lest we die." They repeat the oath and promise in Exodus 24.

What is the significance of this? First, the Israelites distorted what God said and added to it. God said, "Don't touch the mountain or you will die." They said, "If we hear You, we will die." Likewise, legalists always distort and add to God's genuine requirements trying to be holier than what God is requiring at the moment. Second, Israel got God's require-ment, the Law, without the benefit of personal interchange with His voice. Moses got the Person—they got the code. They swore themselves to an oath to which they could not hope to keep. There yet remains a rest for the people of God in relationship to His Person.

When I saw this, not a little of my Christian foundation was shaken, and yet I think it is clear. The center of the Old Covenant was Torah and Torah observance. The Old Covenant is characterized by relationship to a written code and the promise of a Person. The center of the New Covenant is Jesus and Calvary. The New Covenant is characterized by realization of the promise and relationship to the Person revealed to us through the written Word and by the Spirit. The outpouring of the Holy Spirit on the Day of Pentecost was a change in the cosmic order. Jesus said clearly that upon His ascension and glorification there would be a relational change. The relationship He had personally with the Father would be available to His disciples as a result of the Spirit's outpouring (see John 20:17; Acts 1:8; Acts 2).

We must not reduce the New Covenant faith down to mental appre-hension of New Testament facts ("my Scripture's better than your Scripture," etc.). The letter does not characterize the order of this present age. The Spirit characterizes it. The Word reveals a Person (see John 5:38-40). If we master the Word, but miss the Person, we have failed the grace of God and are living in an Old Covenant paradigm even though our "lan-guage" may be New Testament. We are not called to relate to precepts. We are called to relate to a Person who will impart His precepts to our hearts.

Someone who is living his or her Christian life by principle, rather than out of the principle of life, is manifesting a symptom of legalism.

FEARFUL FREEDOM

Another manifestation of legalist disease is a stronghold of fear. Legalists live under the constant and nagging fear of God's rejection as a consequence of disappointing God or "missing His will." They fear the rejection that comes from making a mistake. They live in fear of the punishment for failure or inadequacy that is associated with earthly relationships.

Many believers prefer secure slavery to scary freedom. If someone is a slave, freedom is limited, but life is predictable—meals are regular and tasks the same. A slave knows that if he fulfills certain behaviors the slave master will not wound him. If he behaves, he need not fear the master's whip (assuming a non-pathological master). However, when set free, a slave is now confronted with the reality that to fully engage in life means having the risk of pain that cannot be predicted. When Israel was in bondage in Egypt, they were oppressed and they suffered, but they did not have to go to war. When they were finally delivered, they had to provide their own food and go to war. Freedom results in scars and wounds that we might not be able to control.

Perhaps you have seen the old movies where the slaves are rowing in the bottom of a Roman galley ship. Consider their conditions: fed regularly (though poorly), predictable everyday, job clearly defined (row), stay in rhythm (don't do anything out of the normal), don't distinguish yourself, conform with others—someone else is responsible for the direction of the ship, all you have to do is row. So even though the atmosphere stinks, and the chains chafe your ankles, there are elements that appeal to those who find liberty scary. If the crew should experience a mutiny and overthrow the oppressing captain and slave driver, what would a galley slave experience? A combination of exhilaration and delight. After a few exhilarating gusts of clear air, a paralyzing reality sets in: *I don't know how to steer this thing. All I know how to do is row.*

This is the same dynamic of a legalist. They do not have to exercise any degree of self-determination. They just have to stay in sync with the drumbeat the slave master determines. Their personalities are actually extinguished.

OH FATHER, WHERE ARE YOU?

Much has been written in recent years on the issue of the "father wound" by many able authors, both secular and Christian.[5] They have all done a better job than I possibly can do in this effort, and in far more detail. I am just going to briefly comment on how the issue relates to legalism and performance-based religion. Fatherlessness manifests itself primarily in one of two ways: passive abnegation or striving aggressiveness, and it fits hand in glove with legalism.

I believe that in an ideal family[6] it is primarily a father's responsibility to stamp his children with a sense of identity and purpose. This does not demean the role of mothers or the need for feminine impartation in any way. Moms transfer and impart qualities and values to their children that are equally valuable. In a single-parent situation (male or female) God's grace and the contribution of the diverse gifts of the community of believers can make up for any lack. It is just that when a father has not adequately given his child a place in his heart and affections[7]—a place of belonging, security, love, identity, courage, and safety—the child often grows up trying to please God the Father, who in the individual's mind, is a magnified reflection (for better or worse) of the qualities (or absence thereof) of one's earthly father.

I have heard it said that "the biblical order" is for men to teach boys and men, and for women to teach girls and women. I disagree. Each has something they can offer to the opposite sex. In the Scriptures, the admonition for the elder women to teach or impart to the younger, deals contextually with domestic issues of relationships and responsibilities (see Titus 2:3-5). It says nothing about who is responsible for feminine (or masculine for that matter) psychological development or "soul" issues. It is fathers who have the power to put in or take out courage from the hearts of their children, both genders.[8]

For instance if a young child is learning to ride a bike for the first time and he falls off and seriously hurts himself, a maternal response might be to provide comfort, care, assurance, affection, and the cleaning of wounds—certainly a Christ-like, appropriate, and necessary response. However a paternal or "masculine" love response might be, "Son, let's get on the bicycle again. I am going to help you conquer this thing." If the life-goal is feeling good about oneself and the avoidance of personal pain or discomfort at all costs, then the maternal response alone is adequate. But if the goal is instilling courage to overcome an obstacle that might involve risk and pain, then a masculine touch is needed also. We need healed overcomers, and overcoming healers.

I know, these are generalities, but I think we can see the validity and need for the impartation of what might be called the feminine virtues of tenderness and compassion and the masculine virtues of courage, conquering, overcoming, daring, and fearlessness.[9] One set of qualities is not better than the other; they are complementary according to divine design, and for complete psychological health, both should be present. Courage without compassion is insensitivity. Compassion without courage is cowardliness.

"DADDY, HOW DO I LOOK?"

The importance of a father's impartation can be demonstrated in another simple scenario: a ten-year-old daughter in her first formal dress. After the young girl has put the dress on for the first time she might ask her mother how she looks. Mom might say, "Honey, you look so pretty." That would be a great response.

The daughter might respond, "I wonder what Daddy would think?"

Mom says, "He is in the living room reading the paper; go ask him."

So the daughter goes to the living room and tries to get Daddy's attention. But Daddy is too engrossed with the newspaper and the television and doesn't even bother to turn around to see his daughter. He simply responds without even looking, "Honey, you look fine. If you like it, I like it."

The disheartened daughter presses him for engagement and relational contact, but Dad cannot pull himself away from the immediate object of his attention. The little girl goes back to her Mom who asks, "What did Daddy say?"

Crestfallen, the young girl responds, "He liked it," as she walks back upstairs with something in her heart that had not been there a few minutes earlier: a father wound and the thought, "I am not worthy to be noticed."

In this mini scene, what damage has the father done to the daughter? He has sown a wound and pain into that little girl's heart that might take decades to heal, if it ever does.

Mom may say the dress looks beautiful, but there is nothing like Daddy telling his little girl that she looks beautiful and that she is his princess. If a dad does not provide masculine affirmation free from any overtones of sexuality to his young daughter who is developing a sense of self-awareness for the first time, she will certainly find assurance and identity in the arms of another man when she is 16. Invariably, it seems, the other man comes from the bottom of the barrel of humanity. Many a fine but damaged daughter runs to the arms of a low-life scum who has learned that to get what he wants all he has to do is build the road of personal value and identity into the heart of a woman that was never laid in her soul by her father when she was ten. Unfortunately for the daughter, after the heart is won under false pretenses, the abuse usually follows.

"HAVE FUN STORMING THE CASTLE, BOYS!"[10]

In medieval warfare there were two ways to take a castle: storm it by force or starve it out by siege warfare, cutting off the residents from the vital supplies they need for life. It does not matter much whether the father-wound results from aggressive authoritarianism and (God forbid) abuse of different sorts, or passive disengagement and self-centeredness on the part of a father. Aggressive authoritarianism is like storming the castle. Emotional absenteeism is like cutting the castle off from its vital food supply. The end result is the same: death to the inhabitants, hatred and resentment toward the attacking army (father). Aggressive authoritarianism squelches personality in a subordinate and becomes the seedbed of resentment and rebellion. Passivity and disengagement promotes insecurity and fearfulness. Individuals who have experienced either of these father-wounds will be prone to the appeal of rules and regulations because performance-based religion meets a need in both.

A defiant rebel offers up perfect performance as a means of proving to an abusive or emotionally distant father that he or she doesn't need him anyway. In a sense, even "Christian obedience" becomes a distorted form of rebellion thrown into the face of an aggressive or absent father: "See, Dad, I made it without you and you are an idiot." Rule-keeping and spiritual regulations become the measuring tools of achievement. With every act of obedience or progress a spiritual statement is made: "Dad, I didn't need you then, and I don't need you now."

Healing for the father-wound can be facilitated through appropriate teaching and impartation of sound, New Covenant truth from the moment someone experiences the new birth. By building a new sense of identity and value in Christ immediately in the new convert's life, legalism is cut off "at the pass." However, all teaching, even good teaching, can be nothing more than meaningless philosophy if our teaching is not incarnate in our lives. There is also no substitute for developing a real relationship with a genuine father, naturally or spiritually.

Teaching about fathering and the father-wound is not the same thing as experiencing healing at the hands of not only our Heavenly Father, but also an earthly father. If the hands of a father have wounded us, it will take the hands of another father to heal us. God designs it that way so we cannot hide in our woundedness. He forces us out of hiding and into the place of our pain to heal us. He loves us too much to let us hide in reactionary responses to the wounds of others. We will not participate in His resurrection Calvary life by hiding and denial. We experience resurrection life as we allow Him to go to and touch the deepest pains in our heart.

There is a great responsibility upon the believing community to manifest a spirit of grace at the point of other people's weaknesses, especially the new convert. We are Christ's ambassadors, representing the Father as He did. If we project an incorrect image of the Father upon the new convert, contradicting our pulpit teaching and doctrine, we are setting the new convert up for unnecessary crisis. Surely, the Holy Spirit is able to keep His own. I just do not want to be responsible for making His job more difficult.

"JUST THE FACTS, MA'AM"[11]

There is danger inherent in Christianity: imperfect people pursuing perfection. The pursuit is healthy; but thinking we have arrived at our destination gets a little scary. Individuals manifest different behaviors as they pursue the Christian ideal of being conformed to the image of Christ. One person's ideal version of Christ may bear no resemblance to another's. We will reflect our understanding of the image of God through our temperaments. Redemptively, this becomes the diverse manifestation of the multifaceted character and nature of Christ on earth. Christ is incarnated again through His diverse Body. On the downside, if uncrucified or unsanctified, the God-given personality or temperament can become the manifestation of some very legalistic behavior.

In M. Scott Peck's book *People of the Lie*, he summarizes some qualities of a perfectionist: A perfectionist is someone who has an intense desire to appear good, without moral or social fault at all costs, and to be accepted by others as a result of their perfection or performance. Perfectionists acknowledge the need for spiritual growth, but have psychological aversion to the pain associated with acknowledgment of personal weakness and shortcoming. They unceasingly engage in trying to maintain the appearance of moral or spiritual uprightness and social acceptability. This requires great amounts of emotional, spiritual, and physical energy frequently rendering the perfectionist physiologically fatigued. They are acutely sensitive to social norms and what other people may think. They often have a strong desire to be affirmed, apart from whether or not the facts and circumstances warrant affirmation for a task or job done. They resist scrutiny and measurement from others, especially authority figures, even Christ. Their worst fear is to be found wanting or lacking in someone else's eyes or estimation. They would rather flee from the flawed and imperfect self they understand themselves to be, than to deal with deficiency or lack. They are often compulsive in their behaviors and hard on themselves and others because self-interest requires a pretense of wholeness. Their self-interest requires that everything be "just right" out of the fear that if it is not, their whole universe will break down in some degree or another.

M. Scott Peck also describes the essence of evil in terms that fits the perfectionist (legalist) quite well:

> Utterly dedicated to preserving their self-image of perfection, they are unceasingly engaged in the effort to maintain the appearance of moral purity. They worry about this a great deal. They are acutely sensitive to social norms and what others might think of them…they intensely desire to appear good. Their "goodness" is all on a level of pretense. It is, in effect, a lie…They cannot or will not tolerate the pain of self-reproach. The decorum with which they lead their lives is maintained as a mirror in which they can see themselves righteously reflected…Since they must deny their own badness, they must perceive others as bad…they are men and women of obviously strong will, determined to have their own way. There is remarkable power in the manner in which they attempt to control others.[12]

One might think that describing a "tendency" as evil is a bit strong. But perfectionistic religion has always been the root of murder. In John 7:31 the Scripture relates that "many of the people believed on Him." By John 8:59, the same group of "believers" wanted to kill Him. There are many contextual reasons for the shift of affection (which we will deal with in later chapters), but for our purposes now, suffice it to say that the agitation of the religious perfectionists of the day provoked a spirit of murder that was ultimately manifest at Calvary.

Biblical maturity is not necessarily found in the one who most efficiently executes articulated expectations. That person may be an idealist who cannot live with the tension between pursuing a high Christian call and accommodating personal weakness, failure, and inefficiency in others. A mature Christian has the capacity to absorb the offenses and weaknesses of others, not just demand that they perform up to the code of ideals. Biblical maturity is defined by the relationships we maintain (loving God and loving others), not the rules we keep.

My dear friends of many years, Pastors David and Phyllis Hannon, had a needlepoint in their home that often spoke to me on this issue. I cannot give credit to the original author, as I do not know who it may have been. But it seems to sum up the essence of the danger of idealism and perfectionism.

There Are Two Things: The Actual and the Ideal
[reality and the high call]

Maturity sees the ideal, but lives with [is gracious to] *the actual.*

Failure [passivity] *accepts only the actual and rejects the ideal.*

Accepting only the ideal and refusing the actual is immaturity
[legalism, perfectionism].

Do not criticize the actual because you have seen the ideal
[perfectionists and idealists].

Do not reject the ideal because you have seen the actual
[status quo worshipers].

Maturity [grace and spirit] *is to live with the actual*
but to hold on to the ideal.[13]

Amen. Perfectionism is an Adamic counterfeit of biblical maturity and is itself a symptom of a good case of legal infection.

EXPECT OF OTHERS WHAT YOU EXPECT OF YOURSELF

Right on the heels of perfectionism is the tendency to be demanding. The legalists will either excuse themselves or accuse others. It is amazing to see how people's theology changes when the issue ceases to be abstract but personal. For example, I know of people who railed against the evils of suicide as the ultimate sin, how all those who committed suicide are in hell, etc.—*until* one of their relatives committed suicide and an epiphany of understanding suddenly occurred. Likewise I know those who rail against any hot button issue—divorce and remarriage, abortion, homosexuality, adolescent sexual activity—until someone in their immediate family is touched by the issue and, voila, like Paul on the Damascus road they have an instantaneous theological conversion. I suppose change is better late than never. Growth in understanding and graciousness of spirit can never be too late, but would it not be better if a demanding spirit were not manifest in the first place?

People who have overcome extreme trauma or chronic personal difficulty in their own life often can be very legal. The attitude in these folks can be: "I pulled myself up by my boot straps. I didn't get any help, so what's your excuse?" Demanding folks view life's challenges not as an opportunity to engage God in His Personhood, spirit of revelation, relational discovery, and adventure but rather as just another chapter where one has to exert willpower to overcome whatever dish life has served up.

Sometimes we misunderstand the essence of Christianity as an exercise of the will. Much of what we call Christianity is merely controlled behavior, no more spiritual (Holy Spirit) in its source than what a nonbeliever could do through his or her own strength and determination. Christianity is not about being full of willpower and determination. It is about having a crucified and submitted will, not an energized one. Humanity is made for self-surrender, not self-actualization.

Much of the modern "pop-culture Gospel" is saturated with psychological self-help and self-actualization philosophy dressed in the clerical garb of Christian language. Some of the most evil human beings who ever lived had incredibly strong wills, quite self-actualized, but that did not make them Christian! Sometimes individuals with the strongest wills are the most prone to depression because if they ever get into a situation where their "will resource" fails them, it can be hard for them to bear. Both Napoleon and Hitler, individuals hardly short on will, were prone to depression.

If one's success in the Christian life is the result of the exercise of biblical principles in the power of human will and determination, a strong-willed individual is not too likely to be gracious to a weaker vessel. It is the logical outcome of his or her paradigm. If success is merely due to intellectual apprehension of biblical principle and the exercise of human will, any personal failure in others can only be the result of sloth, laziness, negligence, and weakness that is to be disdained and chastised. If, on the other hand, one's history of Kingdom success has been a series of failures and redemption, brokenness and healing, death and resurrection, wilderness and divine encounter, hopelessness and faith, that individual is far less likely to be demanding of those who at any given moment may be experiencing a situation or circumstance where "bucking up" is as appropriate an expectation as expecting a blind man to describe the color red.

O-OH, SAY CAN YOU SEE, ANY BED BUGS ON ME[14]

Introspection—the self-examination of character flaws—is another manifestation of legalism. There can be a human tendency to worry about and emphasize moral and spiritual trivialities and stamping God's name on them. Social psychologists and behaviorists call it "compensatory conscience"—worrying about minor things in avoidance of major ones. King David manifested compensatory conscience when he adjudged the thief of a lamb worthy of death while excusing his own adulterous and murderous behavior.

The introspective have an over-stimulated conscience. They practice the doctrine of avoidance, focusing on the negative embargoes and bans: Don't do this; don't do that; avoid this; and avoid that. Walking in holiness is not about avoiding sin. It is about receiving life. A dirty cup can't make itself clean by focusing on its dirt. Flush it out, and it will be clean. So it is with the believer.

This tendency is the scourge of deeper life Christianity. This very dangerous propensity is particularly pronounced in those for whom the primary teaching and preaching emphasis is Christian character development. It is the means by which the devil successfully neutralizes thousands of well-meaning believers who genuinely have a passion for Jesus in His Personhood and a deep desire to be conformed to His image. The devil will actually take passion for the pursuit of Jesus Christ and a desire for Christ-likeness and use it against believers to get them in an introspective mode of self-analysis that leads to spiritual paralysis.

The trouble creeps in when we believe that His delight in us is based on our degree of conformity to His image, rather than our past acceptance "in the Beloved." God delights in me because I have been made His own through Christ's work, not mine, and my character conformity is the *fruit* of His delight in me, not the *reason* for His delight in me. This distinction is frequently lost.

In all of the New Testament there is only one passage of Scripture that exhorts the believer to self-examination (see 1 Cor. 11:28-34). The context is partaking of the Lord's Supper: Are you "in the faith"? Even in this passage we must note that the examination is not to take place inwardly and introspectively, but outwardly and relationally. The passage is not about one's personal sanctification, but one's relational connectedness to the Lord and others in the Body. It is our interpersonal relationships that determine worthiness to eat the Lord's Supper, not our personal piety. As surprising as it might be to some, other than that passage there is not a single verse in the New Testament that exhorts a believer to examine oneself in any context.

The reason is simple. We are called to have neither sin-consciousness nor self-awareness. We are called to have Christ-awareness. In Christianity, the Adamic nature is called to death, crucifixion, and extinction, not self-awareness, self-consciousness, and self-management of a spiritual regimen. Self, whether abasing itself or exalting itself, is still self! Groveling or boasting, it is still self! In biblical Christianity, self is called to die daily, not examine itself daily for a pulse. We are not called to be like some spiritual turkey basting in God's oven of spiritual processes that requires a thermometer of self-measurement to be stuck in our souls every couple of hours to see if we are done yet! We are called to a grave not an oven! The Adamic nature's destiny is the grave, not the mirror.

SEEING THE LIGHT

Have you ever been in a rural atmosphere where there are absolutely no lights—no moon and no incident light of a nearby city? If you have, you will know that in such an atmosphere it is impossible to see one's hand in front of one's face. Imagine if I were covered in sores in such an atmosphere. All the self-inspection in the world would be fruitless because I cannot produce enough light to see what I am doing. Trying harder to see more would be futile. More time or more effort will produce nothing but the same results—darkness—because the critical element is missing: *light*.

Now consider if someone should bring a candle into that situation. I would be able to see sores in proportion to the amount of light I have been given. If someone should exchange the candle for a flashlight, I could see more…a flashlight for a floodlight even more…and a floodlight for a 50,000-watt halogen light, even more. *My ability to see is in direct proportion to the light I have been given.* That is the way it is for the believer. We do not possess enough light concerning ourselves in the face of the Word to do self-inspection for sin.

Suppose I am in a place with God that He is dealing with me at a 50,000-watt halogen level. If I am not a walking vessel of grace, what would I expect of others and project on others? Right—50,000 watts. But what if God is only dealing with my brother or sister at a candle level? What right do I have to project on them the level of sanctification that God is dealing with me about? Well, you say, the Bible is the standard. Yes, indeed it is. But Jesus is Lord of the Bible and the Spirit is sovereign over His own. Issues of need, priority, timing, and sequence in the life of a believer is up to His sovereignty in relationship to the believer, not about projecting on someone else the results of my own introspection and self-analysis. This is so vital in our Christian walk. Failure on this point yields so much legalism and relational conflict. Those prone to introspection are manifesting a symptom of legalism.

One of my favorite Scriptures is Psalm 36:9: "In Thy light, we shall see light." The only time any of us is suited to make an evaluative self-judgment about our character development or spiritual progress in the Kingdom is in the light of His illuming presence—when we are in communion with Him, with the Word of God as our base. I am responsible for those issues concerning which the Lord may be dealing with me at any given moment. I am not responsible for those areas of non-Christlikeness that the Lord is not currently bringing up.

YE IS WE

No one is exempt from reading the Scriptures through their own cultural filter as I have discussed elsewhere. As Americans we have a strong filter of individualism that makes us assume that the Bible is written to "me" (rather than the Church), that the promises are "mine" (rather than ours), that salvation happened to me (rather than "I have been brought into the corporate Body"), that spiritual warfare is something *I* enter into (rather than the ascendancy of the corporate "we" of Ephesians 6:12: "*We* wrestle not…"). This tendency, when mixed with an unfortunate grammatical reality of modern English, can result in a very self-centered and individualistic view of what Christianity is all about.

Every Bible translation has its strengths and weaknesses. Translators and interpreters all have to make value judgments, some of which may be better than others. One of the strengths of the Old English of the King James Version that genuinely suffers in modern translations is that in modern English we do not have a pronoun that distinguishes between second person plural and singular. In modern English we use "you" for both. Sometimes only the context can determine if we mean singular or plural and there are times where it is very unclear which is meant, even when considering context.

In many ways, modern English is quite vague in this regard and is inferior to New Testament Greek or Old English. In Old English the distinction was maintained. You singular was "thee" or "thou" and you plural was "ye." It is clearly beyond the scope of this writing to go into detail on this matter, but I would strongly recommend that an excellent study would be to reevaluate some familiar passages of Scripture with a good Greek lexicon at hand and pay particular attention to second person plural and singular uses of "you."

I believe the exercise would demonstrate that the typical American independent, self-aware, and individualistic paradigm of biblical consciousness is not only faulty linguistically, it is faulty culturally, as the Semitic-Mediterranean culture in which the Scriptures were originally written had a corporate consciousness culture, not individualistic.[15] Many of the terms that we routinely associate with Christianity such as truth, knowledge, righteousness, faith, and honor were understood in the context of community and inter-relationship of both the Hebrew and Greek cultures and language, not as individual or private virtues as in our culture. *Any emphasis on personal character development that minimizes the vitality of relationship to God and corporate relational interaction is a betrayal of the Gospel and a manifestation of a legal infection.*

This fact was driven home to me in a revelatory way when I had another one of my foundational belief systems shaken by what the Scriptures say instead of what I thought they said (a common malady)! In Exodus 18 the familiar story of Jethro advising Moses is recounted. Jethro tells Moses to pick out a certain quality of leader to help him administer leadership responsibilities over Israel. The leaders should be:

• Able men, men of personal resource, wealth, valor, and strength

- God-fearers

- Men of truth

- Haters of covetousness

Now, that's a pretty good list of character traits! However, how many of these fine individuals made it into their inheritance? *Zero.* Why? They were in the same group of people in Exodus 19 and 20 who opted to avoid relationship with God, choosing instead to make a covenant oath to obey His principles. They missed divine encounter and got the code. *Our personal character development is not the guarantee by which we will inherit God's promises in our lives.*

UNCONSCIOUS TO SIN

Another key passage that could help the introspective legalist is Hebrews 10:2. The author of the epistle boldly states that if there could have been a once and for all sacrifice for sin in the Old Covenant era, the result would have been "no more conscience of sin." This sounds so utterly radical as to make one wonder how such a thing could be, but it is exactly the point the author of Hebrews is making. In Christ's sacrifice such an incredible thing has happened, once and for all. Our conscience has been purged. Sin has been purged, not merely covered and atoned for, but purged, washed away.

It is unfortunate that there is much lyric content in contemporary worship choruses that, although they may be beautiful melodically and easy to sing, contain very poor theology. The danger in this is that bad theology gets reinforced on the wings of a pretty melody in the minds of the singer. The first century heretic, Arius, knew this and used it to great effect by putting his doctrine to the tunes of popular bar songs and sailors' melodies that were easily singable and memorable by the common people. His doctrine may have been poor, but his marketing was excellent.[16]

One such shame is the reference in many songs of a contemporary flavor that refer to Jesus' blood "covering" our sin. It may come as a shock, but there is not a single New Testament reference to such a thing.[17] Yes, dear reader. No such verse exists. The concept of covering sin belongs to the Old Covenant. There is no basis in New Testament doctrine to refer to our sins being covered. Covering is an appropriate Old Testament image of temporariness. Sin that is covered is still present, but hidden. Sin that is purged no longer exists. The appropriate New Covenant metaphors are those of removal, not covering, and the apostolic authors assiduously and precisely never refer to our sins as being covered. Through Jesus' sacrifice, our sins have been purged,[18] washed,[19] and cleansed,[20] *not* covered.

The author of Hebrews contrasts the Old Covenant sacrifices, which could never purge a conscience completely, with Christ's sacrifice. A believing Israelite's assurance had to be renewed each year on the Day of Atonement and the Israelite never knew if the sins he or she had committed were forgiven until the High Priest successfully came out of the Holy of Holies on that day. The Old Covenant believer had to live every day with an abiding consciousness of sin and a *hope* that it *would be* forgiven. The New Covenant believer is not to have an abiding consciousness of sin, but rather an abiding consciousness of Christ and the assurance not only of sins forgiven, but sins purged.

In the New Covenant there has been a tremendous change of consciousness. Prior to Calvary and Pentecost, the center of spiritual consciousness was Torah (the Law) and Law observance. Paul rightly points out that the law can illumine sin but it does not deliver from sin. Since Pentecost, for the believer, there is to be a new center of consciousness, the indwelling Spirit of Christ. I am responsible only for those character issues that the indwelling Spirit brings to my consciousness through the revelation of the Word. Failure to understand this will result in a type of Christianity that is obsessed with the discovery of blemishes.

How could such a perversion exist among God's people? Through an over-emphasis on personal character and responsible Christian living energized by a legalistic spirit.

NO CONDEMNATION—REALLY, NONE

The glorious news is found in Romans 8:1. After Paul spends considerable time in Romans 6 explaining our identification with Christ in His death and resurrection, he shifts into the controversial[21] passage of Romans 7 where he discusses the flesh-spirit struggle. The passage then crescendos in Romans 8:1, which reads: "There is therefore now no condemnation to them which are in Christ Jesus, who walk not after the flesh, but after the Spirit."

Gotcha! That is not what the Scripture says. Romans 8:1 is one of those passages that has been seriously corrupted by generations of well-meaning scribes who themselves could not believe how good the good news is. Notice that in the King James Version quoted above, the promise is conditional upon the believer's behavior. If you behave properly then there is no condemnation, but if you do not, the implication is that there *is* condemnation. In other words, you had better behave, or you can expect to be condemned.

The best conservative scholarship and manuscriptural evidence supports the following reading: "no condemnation." There are no qualifiers! For the believer who is in Christ (see Rom. 6) and who experiences the struggle of Romans 7, condemnation has been removed through a fiat decree of the Father and an act of Christ.

The process of endless self-examination and introspection will result in either pride in a sense of self-accomplishment, or despair and depression in a sense of inadequacy and failure. Both are carnal Adamic responses that do not belong in the heart of a believer.

GUILT AND SHAME

Slavery's shackles have served as a metaphor for sin throughout the life of the Church. In Romans 6, Paul says that we were bond slaves to sin prior to our conversion. Bill Gaither's classic worship chorus, *He Touched Me*, starts with this line: "Shackled by a heavy burden." In the natural, it was very common for those who had been slaves for a long period of time to have open wounds on their ankles from the constant chafing of the shackles. Removing the shackles did not immediately heal the wounds. Eventually the wounds would heal, but would often leave a scar.

A wound and a scar are similar in that both are reminders of a historical event or condition. The difference is that a wound still has pain associated with it, but a scar does not. Christians set themselves up for some unnecessary difficulties with an expectation that when God "makes all things new" we have the right and expectation of no scars. In Christ, we are not promised a scar-less existence.[22] We are promised that He took our pain. Often, the place of our past brokenness, our scarring, becomes the very platform for the resurrection life of Christ to be manifest in effective ministry.

Forgiveness of sin and restoration to right standing and fellowship with God is like the removal of the binding shackles. But just like the natural, there is an issue that often lingers and requires healing even after the experience of forgiveness of sin. An abiding sense of shame and unworthiness often torments God's children after conversion. Just as the sores on a slave's ankle serve as a constant reminder of a past of slavery, shame attempts to work the same way in a believer's psychology. Shame is the constant awareness of one's moral indebtedness to past sin. It is like the devil's phylactery: a constant reminder to your mind's eye of your past slavery in sin. The connection between a psychology of shame and performance-based religion is as old as the Garden of Eden.

In Genesis 3:10-12, Adam's response to his failure has five components:[23]

1. *Fear*—"I was afraid" (Gen. 3:10).

2. *Shame*—"I was naked" (Gen. 3:10).

3. *Control/Self-Initiation*—"I hid myself" (Gen. 3:10).

4. *Failure*—God's inquiry accentuates Adam's sense of failure (see Gen. 3:11).

5. *Accusation/Blame*—"the woman You gave me" (see Gen. 3:12).

Adam's response to the psychological condition of shame, fear, and self-awareness of deficiency or fault is to take self-initiation to address the situation (the fig leaf) and to shift the blame to God and his wife. Shame remains a powerful ally of an accusing legalistic spirit. To fully examine the implications of this fivefold stronghold would take us beyond the scope of this writing. Suffice it to say here that we can see the shame/self-initiation/performance link has continued to manifest itself in humanity ever since the Garden.

Some forms of theology ("worm theology") actually encourage the believer to focus on his or her "wormy" condition before a holy God. The basis of the theology, not surprisingly, is taken from the Old Testament (see Ps. 22:6; Isa. 41:14). It is important that we differentiate between a Holy Spirit sense of guilt and a tormenting spirit of shame. While both the Old and New Testaments used a variety of different Hebrew and Greek words for shame, the New Testament Scriptures do not explicitly use the term *guilt* or *guilty*. The Holy Spirit's ministry is, in part, to bring conviction of sin (see John 16:8). Having a Holy Spirit sense of conviction of sin is a healthy thing if it is wrought out of communion with the same Spirit, not just the arid demands of the Word resulting from introspection. However, believers often struggle with a deep sense of unworthiness, valuelessness, and

shame that is not the same as conviction from God, but in our mind or soul it can often feel like it is, or masquerade like it is.

Indeed, in our flesh dwells no good thing, but my Christianity is not made effective by focusing on my Adamic worminess, but through the acknowledging, reckoning, believing in, and manifesting of Christ in me. The effectiveness of my faith is accomplished not by introspection and sin inventory, but by "the acknowledging of every good thing which is in [me] in Christ Jesus" (Philem. 6). Focusing on one's unworthiness will result in a plaguing sense of shame.

What then is the difference? Guilt has to do with transgression and failure for things done or omitted—sins of omission or commission—*things* I have done wrong. Shame is a condition that makes me feel like there is something wrong with *me* in my personhood and identity. Conviction and guilt for sin that comes from the Holy Spirit is always accompanied with a sense of hope. It is never accompanied by a sense of personal rejection and separation from God. The Holy Spirit never convicts and leaves the believer with a sense of abandonment, isolation, rejection, powerlessness, and hopelessness. Any sin awareness that is unaccompanied by divine intimacy and a great revelation of Christ's sufficiency for the sin is not from God. Shame is the devil's counterfeit for conviction.

So far, I have introduced and defined a problem, demonstrated why it is a problem (its appeal), and what some of the symptoms of the problem are. Diagnosis is over! Aren't you glad? Sometimes focusing on a problem can leave one feeling overwhelmed or hopeless. If that is the case for you, great! I have succeeded! It means you are ready for remedy!

I have some good news and some bad news. I have a remedy, but I can't give it to you. If I were to lay out three or five neatly packaged principles that you could exercise to overcome legalism, I would be betraying my own emphasis in this writing! There is no substitute for the relational experience of knowing Him in the power of His resurrection and the fellowship of His suffering. This cannot be reduced to an easy-to-follow procedure. I can't schedule an appointment with God for you. I can't program your burning bush experience. Kingdom advance, spiritual growth and development, maturity, etc., are not gained through the acquisition and exercise of principles, but by the experience of dying daily and experiencing His resurrection life (see John 12:24).

Kind of unsatisfying, isn't it? Our old Adamic nature just screams for "an answer" that it can manage—step one, two, three: have problem, add water, bake 15 minutes, and pull out a tray of spiritual victory. It may sound cliché, but Christ is the answer.

Hoping that the gray in my beard means I have gotten a little wiser and not just older, I want to give some bulleted outline features of what God's deliverance for you might look like, what you can expect "in Him" as He leads you out of the chains of legalism and performance-based religion. Admittedly, some of what I have written, and will write, is from my subjective experience. I bear the healed scars on my own ankles of a former slave who has been set free. I invite you to join me in the liberty that is ours in Christ.

There is a common theme in what follows: our acceptance in the Beloved. It's easy to read, simple to confess, but a bit more mysterious to realize and appropriate—to let the truth of it sink deep into our souls and bring experiential healing to our psychology and identity—but that's the short version of exactly what has to happen. Let's review the symptoms and give a brief summary of God's remedy as we anticipate what follows in Part II.

1. Insecurity

I have assurance in the Son (Eph. 1:6).

I am accepted in Him.

I can experience His love even when I fail.

2. Principled Living

Christ is my life, not principled living (Col. 3:4).

He has given me His life freely (Rom. 3:24; 8:32; 1 Cor. 2:12; John 7).

I have a new life source, not a new set of principles (John 7:38; Jer. 31; Heb. 7–8).

There is a revelation of the New Covenant (Jer. 31; Ezek. 36; Heb. 7–8).

3. Fear

Assurance in the Son (Eph. 1:6).

Acceptance (Eph. 1:6).

The revelation of His perfect love toward me (1 John 4:18; John 17:23).

4. Fatherlessness

The comfort of the Person of the Holy Spirit (John 14:16).

He has not left us as orphans (John 14:18).[24]

I am loved by the Father as much as He loves the Son (John 17:23).

5. Perfectionism and Idealism

God will exhaust me. He will take me to places where I cannot succeed (Eph. 2:8-9).

I will experience the crucifying work of His cross that I might learn to freely receive His grace (Gal. 2:20; 1 Cor. 15:10).

6. Demanding

I will sow in mercy that I might reap the same (Matt. 5:7).

God will allow me to fail miserably, exhausting my own strength, to teach me at an experiential level that it is truly His grace and life that sustain me (Gal. 2:20; 1 Cor. 15:31).

When I see how He accepts me even when I fail, in an undemanding way, I will be quick to give mercy to others (Matt. 5:7).

7. Introspection

Christ is my new consciousness. In union with Him, He is the center of my personality and identity (Heb. 10:2; 1 Cor. 6:17).

I develop an active friendship with the person of the Holy Spirit and relate to God as a friend not as a chief inspector (John 15:15).

8. Condemnation

Experiencing His grace and acceptance in the midst of personal failure sets me free like nothing else can (Eph. 2:8-9; Rom. 8:1).

9. Guilt and Shame

Understanding I am cleansed of my sin, not covered (Heb. 13; 10:2, 22; 2 Pet. 1:9).

Acceptance in the Beloved (Eph. 1:6).

CHAPTER FOUR

End Notes

1. The Three Stooges, *Men in Black*, Columbia Pictures, © 1934.

2. A view that is often buttressed by televangelists. I know they mean well trying to argue for the eternal relevancy of God's Word, with which I totally agree. However, the Bible is more than a ninth grade algebra book with the answers in the back for every perplexity life provides. It is the revelation of a Person and the revealing of that Person's Kingdom. For example, my friends David and Phyllis Hannon had a counseling situation in which a young, attractive girl in the fellowship—prayer warrior, faithful over many years, a worshiper—came to them for pre-marriage counseling. She was attracted to another fine young man in the fellowship and wanted to know if she had to tell her prospective husband that when she was 16 she had undergone a sex change operation and had actually been born a male. Yes, God's grace will reach "even people like that" and you won't find a Bible verse to cover things like that. One better have some "Holy Ghost on tap." Rigid rule-following Christians are utterly ill-equipped to meet the needs of humanity of the 21st century and the situations that are outside of tidy little boxes of theology.

3. Most heresy happens when individuals push to the logical extreme either pole of an antinomy. Western intellect has difficulty living with an antinomy.

4. Erwin R. McManus, *An Unstoppable Force: Daring to Be the Church God Has in Mind* (Loveland: Group Publishing, 2001), p. 82.

5. Robert Bly, John Eldredge, Gordon Dalbey, Ed Cole, Paul Vitz, and others.

6. God's grace manifested directly and through the agency of the Body of Christ is more than enough to make up for any lack in those whose family experience was not ideal. In fact, in many ways there is no such thing as an ideal family or an ideal father. We all just have varying degrees of dysfunction, some worse than others.

7. The white, Anglo-Saxon, Protestant virtue of getting up every day and working hard to put bread on the table is not the same thing as making room for your children in your heart. The "provider equals love" ethic was bankrupt in the 1950s and remains bankrupt today. It is the root cause of much alienation between fathers and children. It is also the root of much of the anti-male and anti-authority spirit prevalent in our culture. A child will ultimately despise the emotionally absent but faithful provider father. The emotionally present father who also provides will build a bond that lasts beyond the grave.

8. "Fathers, provoke not your children to anger, lest they be discouraged" (Col. 3:21). The Greek word translated "discouraged" means to break the spirit, remove life's passion, to crush. The English word "discouragement" has as its root the French word for the heart (*coeur*). Dis-"cour"-age-ment is to take away the heart—a metaphor for the robbing of a sense of purpose or the inward ability to overcome with purpose. Aimlessness and a lack of direction in a human being can often be attributed to "fathering" issues.

9. Our politically correct society and extreme feminists would disagree with me. Some feminist Harvard professors believe masculinity is the root of all human woes. See Joyce Milton, *Malpsychia*, pp. 228-29, 256-57.

10. Billy Crystal in *The Princess Bride*, © 1987 MGM Home Entertainment, Act III Communications, a Reiner/Scheinman production.

11. Quote made famous by Sergeant Joe Friday from the show Dragnet.

12. M. Scott Peck, *The People of the Lie* (New York: Touchstone, 1983) pp. 71-77.

13. Parenthetical comments are mine.

14. The playground lyrics for the *Star-Spangled Banner*, with apologies to Francis Scott Key.

15. See Malina and Rohrbaugh, *Social Science Commentary of the Synoptics and Social Science Commentary of the Gospel of John.*

16. During the Christological controversies of the fourth century, Arius set the following lyrics to melody: "There was a time when the Son was not" to support his doctrine that Christ was generated in time from the Father, that the Logos did not have eternal existence.

17. The interested and ambitious reader is encouraged to pursue a New Testament word study with a good concordance or computer program and discover that this is indeed accurate.

18. Heb. 13; 10:2; 2 Pet. 1:9.

19. Heb. 10:22; 1 Cor. 6:11; Rev. 7:14; Titus 3:5; Eph. 5:26.

20. Acts 11:9; John 15:3.

21. Differing opinions exist as to whether or not Paul refers to his own experience, pre- or post-conversion, or if he is speaking hypothetically.

22. For example: Jacob's limp, Paul's wounds.

23. I am indebted to Dr. Chester and Rev. Betsy Kylstra of Proclaiming His Word Ministries, *Restoring the Foundations Manual*, for germinal thought in regard to this stronghold. Used with permission.

24. The word translated "comfortless" is the Greek *orphanos*: orphaned, abandoned, bereft, fatherless.

CHAPTER FIVE

Paying Off the Creditor

Teaching from Old Testament typology can be dangerous. Typology is like the overactive thyroid of the Kingdom. When over producing, the results frequently do not have any resemblance to solid New Testament exegesis! Sound New Testament exegesis needs to be the guide. I try to maintain a few vital interpretive principles when I preach or teach from Old Testament types and shadows:

- The Scriptures testify of Christ. He is the substance and reality of all Old Testament Scriptures (John 5:37-42; Heb. 1–13).

- We must read the Old Covenant with a spirit of life, liberty, and grace. New Covenant light illumines Old Covenant letter, not the other way around.

- The cross of Christ is the great interpretive act and instrument. It is the filter through which we must understand the Old Covenant. Some precepts from the Old Covenant era "pass through" Calvary into the New Covenant era, others do not.

- Old Covenant typology must have a solid New Testament exegetical counterpart in explicit apostolic doctrine to be valid for and binding upon the New Covenant believer.

Using these interpretive principles to reign in flights of spiritual fancy, we will go on a verse-by-verse excursion of Second Kings 4:1-7: the account of the widow and the cruse of oil. Sometimes when people study this story they emphasize the miraculous provision of oil but they overlook the circumstances leading up to the supernatural provision.

The main players in the scene are the indebted widow, her sons, and the creditor. Because of the death of her godly husband and provider, she is unable to pay her bills. The "repo" man has come to make his claim. Rather than towing off her late-model chariot, which she can no longer afford, he is coming to take her sons into slavery to work off their father's debt.

The creditor has the legal and moral right to demand that the widow pay what is owed. She is in a self-induced state of indebtedness. Colossians 2:14 describes us as willingly "signing on" to the terms and conditions of the law.[1] In Romans 7:12 and First Timothy 1, Paul makes it clear that the law is just, good, and holy. The problem is not with the law, but with our complete inability to live up to the covenant we agreed to in Adam. This is exactly like the widow facing the creditor knocking on her door: a legitimate, self-inflicted state of moral, financial, and legal indebtedness, and no ability to pay.

No Tenure

The widow is neither a sinner (Gentile, outside of God's covenant) nor a spiritual novice. She is the wife of one of God's "junior prophets," likely an acquaintance of Elisha's,[2] and perhaps Elijah's. She and her husband were familiar with a spirit-life that had a quality beyond the routine liturgical elements of the temple. They had familiarity with the supernatural elements of the faith, particularly the prophetic voice of the Lord.

Neither our maturity nor the confession of God's promises immunizes us from life's perplexing circumstances and struggles. Rather, the Old and New Testament Scriptures[3] link glory and maturity with suffering. This is definitely not a popular topic in today's church climate. You won't get invitations to speak at the "Global Victory Conference" if you emphasize suffering. However, it is an unfaithful mishandling of God's Word to minimize or deny this reality.

I am concerned over a concept of spiritual maturity that equates "success" with how many struggles one avoids through the clever quotation and application of Scriptural principles. It is a theology that puts inordinate emphasis on the blessing of ease, comfort, and material things. Surely, such things are blessings, but their presence or lack does not define blessedness. Jesus and Paul were blessed mightily yet were a tad short on ease and material comfort. It is almost as if we manipulate God with His own Word. He is Prince over His principles. He governs His

Word.[4] One does not extort the King with His own decrees. One submits to the King and asks Him to administrate those decrees that are relevant at the moment for His *eternal purposes.* Much of contemporary mass media Christianity is little more than pop culture, self-help, "you can be a success" philosophy, dressed up in Christian verbiage, not the revelation of Jesus Christ and His cross.

I am not endorsing a self-flagellating, degrading, failure-spirit faith that sanctifies misery, defeat, and sickness in the name of holiness. Rather, the Holy Spirit, as the Spirit of Christ the Lord, is Superintendent of our lives. He can custom arrange circumstances to suit His purposes. The type, degree, and timing of our suffering are up to Him, but every believer will experience something that can be broadly called suffering.[5] Christian maturity is not determined by how success-ful and problem-free one's life is. Christian maturity is defined by the measure of the daily death, fellowship of His suffering, and participa-tion in His resurrection life we experience, which empowers us to love God and love others.

There may come seasons in all of our lives, in the perfect will of God, where the struggle we face could be utterly unrelated to anything we may have done or not done. The situation can be completely beyond our control. There can be eternal issues at stake, which we simply can-not see. There are simply some things that we cannot see or understand from our temporal perspective. To think that we have enough insight to extort God to act by demanding He fulfill His promises *when* we think He ought to, and *how* we think He ought to, is to me not only arrogant, but also shortsighted.

We may not be delivered from a situation. We may be delivered through it (see Heb. 11:33-38). The devil brings guilt and failure into the mind of believers in seasons of difficulty. He causes them to think that if they had just been more diligent, more careful, more spiritual, more obedient, etc., that they would have avoided the present difficulty. This is legalistic and performance-based bondage. One's circumstantial struggle may indeed be related to issues of disobedience, however, it is never categorically so. Discernment is required.

Ministry experience, like our character, also does not immunize us from the demands of the creditor-legalism. It is a strange oxymoron of the Kingdom that the most experienced believers and leaders are often the most vulnerable to legalism. Christian ministry, the pastorate, professional clergy, whatever one wants to call it, is fertile ground for legalism and performance-based religion because of the pressure to succeed and because of peer pressure.

It does not matter whether the slave-driving taskmaster is the internal psychology of the insecure and unvalidated minister, or if it is the demand of the impersonal denominational hierarchy, the pressure to "produce" and the unbearable weight of being a failure crushes ministers with a paralyzing sense of inadequacy and failure. If the evil one can oppress God's leaders with a paralyzing sense of inadequacy, he will neutralize them for Kingdom service. I have personally known individuals who were beaten up and abused by an unrecognized legalistic spirit who are no longer in the ministry—and some are not even serving the Lord at all.

THE CREDITOR'S KNOCK

The law is God's bill collector. It constantly calls attention to our moral indebtedness to God: how much we owe and our obligation to pay. It does little good to curse the bill collector. He is just the representative of Someone who has a legal claim. Our problem is with the legitimacy of God's demand of righteousness upon us, not His agent or revealer of the demand: the law. In the Second Kings 4 passage, the creditor's just demands are about to destroy the widow's family just like the demands of the law slay us because of our iniquity—our moral indebtedness. Legalism demands we perform and measure up. Many believers, including those in fivefold ministry, are like the widow trying to meet the demands of the creditor. It is hopeless. As Paul says with such pathos at the end of Romans 7, "Who shall deliver me...?"

Perhaps you are not sure what the creditor's knock sounds like on the door of your heart and mind. Here are some samples of what the creditor's voice might sound like to you:

- God can't use you because there is sin in your life.

- You failed, so your testimony is ruined.

- Your marriage is bad, your behavior is poor, and God can never use you.

- What are people going to think? What will the leaders think?

- If I am honest about my problem, they will take away my ministry and my position.

- I am the only Christian with this problem. No one understands.

- You can't testify. You are in defeat in that area yourself.

- You've tried and tried and failed. Why do you think you have anything to say?

- You promised you wouldn't, and you did; now God is through with you.

- If you don't obey God quickly and precisely, He will reject you and find someone else who will.

- God is punishing you for your sin.

- God is angry with you. You are getting what you deserve.

DOUBLE JEOPARDY

In biblical numerology, the number two is the number of testimony and witness.[6] The creditor was after the widow's two sons to put them into slavery. One thing legalism does is ruin one's testimonial effectiveness. If believers constantly live under a cloud of failure and self-measurement, they will not have inner psychological impulsion to testify of Jesus. The ever-looming sense of their imperfections acts like a mental anchor that keeps the ship of testimony in dock. They are afraid someone will discover a deficiency in their Christian character and walk, thereby opening themselves up to charges from the unbeliever of "hypocrite."

We need to testify of His perfections, not ours—His redeeming hope, not the process of our sanctification. If we exercise humility and repentance, even our failures and inconsistencies can be the ground for effective testimony to the unbeliever. We need a Savior just like the person we are witnessing to. Legalists come across like know-it-all scolds, pointing out the other person's moral indebtedness, while presuming their own moral perfections. The sanctimonious hypocrite that offends the unbeliever is the one who gives off the aroma of superiority in his or her words and life. The contrite lover of Jesus, winsome and inviting in their spirit, honest and repentant in their failures, is often a refreshing change of diet to what the church normally serves up for unbeliever consumption.

In a Gospel-fatigued culture of smarmy televangelists, unbelievers are not interested in how right and holy we may be. They want to see genuineness. They have a right to demand it. They have a God-given right to "taste us" to see if we are the real thing or not (see Ps. 34:8). Our taste is determined by our genuineness, not our perfections.

Legalism will also steal your fruitfulness, your Kingdom productivity. The widow's children represent her fruitfulness. They are the proof of her legitimate union with her husband. When a man and woman unite in marriage they form a new identity: a "one-flesh entity." For believers, even in the presence of our deficiencies, we have a union with a Heavenly Husband who has sealed our marriage covenant with His own blood. We have received a new name and a new identity as a result of our union with Him. My fruitfulness stems from my union *with* and identity *in* Him, not from the development of my character.

The creditor-devil-legalism always assaults us at the point of our union and new identity. If he can get us to doubt either one, move from them, or live apart from their reality, he has succeeded in luring us with his bait. He tries to get us to believe that our Kingdom fruitfulness is contingent upon how "spot free" we are rather than from the indwelling Christ.

I am fruitful because I am in Him and He in me. My union with my Heavenly Husband is legitimate even though my behavior may be inconsistent. I will not let the creditor-law take my fruitfulness from me. We are promised abundant fruitfulness in the *presence* of our enemies, not in their absence (see Ps. 23:5). The enemies of my own character weaknesses and failures do not negate His promise.

HELP! I NEED SOMEBODY, HELP! NOT JUST ANYBODY![7]

In her distress, the widow does something that has significant bearing for the New Testament believer: She calls to Elisha for help. This has a twofold application. First, she "objectified" her problem—she reached out for help. Second, she responded relationally by reaching out to the "spiritual father" with whom she and her husband had relationship.

Everyone needs someone to whom they relate in an intimate and real way—a spiritual father or mother to turn to when in a life situation for which there are no apparent answers or pathway of escape. Much has been written in recent years on the subject of spiritual fathering and mentoring. This text is not about that subject, other than to say that I agree with its necessity, though I think the form still needs some development and refinement to avoid some legalistic pitfalls.

Paying Off the Creditor

The curse of American Protestantism is individuality and independence. The "Jesus and me" syndrome is a cancer in our church culture. The Scriptures so clearly speak of "a people," a corporate entity: the "let us" of the exhortations of Hebrews. An isolated individualist who says he loves the Lord but not the Lord's people is a deluded religionist. How can an individual separate himself from the ones the Lord plainly declares Himself to be in union with? The objection is usually made that the individual is united with the mystical, metaphysical, universal Church, but not any local assembly. Of course, the rationale is lame as Hebrews clearly admonishes us to not forsake gathering together, literally, *episunagoge*, the synagoging of ourselves.

The fleshing out of Christianity—the experience of hurts, wounds, and offenses and the practice of repentance—is only possible in a covenant community, not the mystical invisible Bride Church. The log-cabin isolationist with an anti-authority chip on his shoulder toward the "organized" church may adhere to a form of Christian philosophy, but he is not a Christian without participation in a local assembly. Such a one is none of Christ's.

As Americans we are so private in our paradigms and so "wounded" from, and resentful toward, authority figures that we are reluctant to reach out to others for help. Sometimes we are comfortable reaching out horizontally to peers when looking for comfort or help, but the real deliverance anointing comes when we reach "up," so to speak, to those who have oversight. We have to reach out to someone who values our future more than our friendship—someone who not only will provide comfort, but will also lead us to that place of discomfort, confrontation, and spiritual growth. Normally a peer friend is inadequate in this regard.

J. Konrad Hölé has insights regarding why an objective, overseeing mentor is important[8]:

- Mentors do not accommodate your present; they help you leave it.

- You will repeat your past until someone who has conquered his or her past speaks unto you.

- The difference between a mentor and a friend is that a friend loves you for what you are, but a mentor loves you for what you can become.

Sometimes the fact that leaders have hurt us is raised as an excuse to not seek objective overseeing influence in our lives. J. Konrad Hölé and Juanita Bynum have a few choice words for that line of thinking.

- It is one thing to be hurt by a wrong mentor; it's another thing to use them as an excuse to not pursue the right one.[9]

- The person who is in position to advance you to the next level is probably the person you get an offense with.[10]

Perhaps some are comfortable objectifying their problems with God in the sense of reaching out and up to Him for help. Yet even in that response, we are sometimes legalistic. The question is, how do we run to God for help? Many believers approach God out of a lack of confidence and with fear, like a beggar who is uncertain of his or her standing. Imagine a father who has given his son a bicycle as a gift for his birthday. Every day the son approaches the father and asks if it is all right if he rides the bike. To make things worse, every time the child approaches the father he is weeping and pleading with his father, begging him for permission to ride the bike. How would a natural father respond in such a situation? Would he be pleased or confused? Of course, it would almost hurt the father, as the father has demonstrated his predetermination for the son to ride by the fact that he has given the child the bike in the first place!

So often when we approach God we approach like that child. Uncertain and insecure we act like if we beg, plead, and weep enough we somehow constrain a reluctant God to release a blessing unto us. When we approach the Lord, we need to approach on the grounds of our favor in Christ, not on the grounds of our self-awareness of deficiency. God is on our side (see Rom. 8:31).

THANKS FOR NOTHING! (2 KINGS 4:2A)

In the presence of the widow's pressing and distressing need, we need to pay attention to what the man of God does for her...*nothing*. *Well,* one might say, *what's the point of reaching out for help if all you get is nothing?*

Not only does Elisha do nothing, but he also asks a stupid question: "What do you have in the house?" What a ridiculous question. The reason she is seeking the man of God in the first place is because she has nothing! I can hear her now: "Thanks a lot. I reach out for help, you give me nothing, then you ask a stupid question and put a demand on me I can't answer. Thanks so much for your help!"

Actually Elisha did what every honorable spiritual person or mentor should do. He caused her to look within for resources. He didn't immediately perform some wonder to relieve the pressure on her life. In some spiritual climates there is an unhealthy dependency on the man of God or counselor as source of supernatural supply or relief. In fact, some authors even proclaim that a mediating class of individuals is *required* by God to obtain complete fullness, victory, and blessing.[11] There can be a temptation in the ministry to be the answer for individuals in need rather than pointing the person to Jesus. It can be psychically addicting to have people dependent on you for supernatural resource.

It is also significant to note that Elisha's response to the widow was not to exhort her to work harder to overcome the situation. Working harder is the legalistic response to every need: work harder, try more, weep longer, pray more, fast more. ***One cannot overcome the demand of the law by being more demanding!*** Elisha forced her to look on what she didn't have. In a sense, she has nothing, but in another sense, she is about to discover what she really has.

A BARREL FULL O' NUTTIN'

When asked by Elisha, the widow downplays what she has in the house (see 2 Kings 4:2b). She says she has "nothing," except a small cruse of oil. Well, *nothing* and *a small cruse of oil* are not the same thing! She had something! She just believed it was inadequate.

How do we respond to God or our leaders when a demand or request is made upon us? Just like the widow did. What do we have in our house? Oh nothing, just a little oil, the eternal *dunamis* Spirit of God living in us. We focus on our lack, need, and deficiency and think that by spiritual begging (falsely called *prayer*) we can squeeze some resources out of God. A spirit of false humility, an obsessing preoccupation with our deficiencies, has *got to go* if we expect to overcome a performance-based spirit. God knew we were worthless in Adam when He saved us, and He knows we are worthless in Adam now, but we are not worthless in Christ. The life of the Son in us is the basis of all God's interactions with us. The indwelling Spirit of the Son of God is the ground of access for a holy God with His creation. The key to victory is the faith appropriation of the reality of the indwelling Spirit.

By Second Kings 4:3, Elisha still hasn't done anything to relieve the widow's situation. Rather than doing some great wonder and rushing to the widow's rescue, Elisha put another requirement on her.

How frustrated we can become with God and God's leaders! We feel betrayed, hurt, and let down. After all, we expected *ministry* to our woundedness from God's leader, not a demand! How harsh!

Ah, but what is the nature of the requirement? It is the requirement of obedient faith. The widow had to act on the unseen. It is no different for us. It is faith that we need, not greater effort. Belief followed by action will determine the rest of the story. If you will not exercise faith, you will never get the creditor off your back. You will just keep trying harder and harder to please God with your own resources and you will experience all the stress and frustration associated with it. Our work is to believe into Christ and yield to His life (see John 6:29).

EXPOSED

Elisha cranks it up another notch and still no supernatural supply! He puts another demand for faith action upon her: "Go borrow not a few of thy neighbors' vessels" (see 2 Kings 4:3). Now this is piling on! What good is it to gather more of what is already empty? Add empty to empty and you get…empty! How frustrating it is for us when we expect God (or the leader in our life) to come riding in to rescue us from some distress or difficulty and instead we are told to do something that, to our natural understanding, seems irrelevant to our need.

The widow's deliverance hinged not only upon her approaching the man of God, objectifying her faith, looking within, but she also had to ***get involved with others around her***. In so doing, she *exposed her lack to her neighbors*. She could have responded to the demand like most of us would: "Why do I have to do that? Why don't you just do a miracle? Why do I have to get others involved?" Fortunately for her, the widow didn't respond like an American Christian.

Here is a picture of the importance of being rightly related and engaged with the body of believers around us. Her deliverance hinged on her willingness to engage with others. So much of our American version of Christianity is a corrupt distortion. We cling to our right to privacy as if it were the 11th commandment. We have distorted a personal relationship with the living God into a *private* relationship with a god configured after our own desires and cultural values. The former is biblically accurate, the latter is not.

It is easy to expect God to do some supernatural wonder. It is much more difficult to believe that God's provision for my deliverance is incarnated in another believer. This is the entire premise of First Corinthians 12–14. Beyond all debate about the continuance of the gifts of the Spirit, the great theme of this passage is this: The provision is in the Body, and relationship with the Body determines even life and death issues (see 1 Cor. 11:28-32).

One of the reasons we do not see supernatural manifestations in the Church in the West like we would hope is our insistence on individualism, isolation, and independence contrary to a covenantal and community ethic that underlies the Scriptures. We think the minister in the pulpit is "wonderful and gifted" but the believer sitting next to us is, well, just like us, empty and not worth pursuing. "Lord, that person doesn't have anything for me. Why do I have to expose my need to my neighbor? I want the 'preacher' to pray for me." We need to see our fellow members as anointed ministers, literal extensions of Christ in the earth. Our supernatural provision might be sitting right next to us.

The principle of corporate relationship as it relates to deliverance and healing is seen also in James 5:13-20: the anointing with oil for the sick. Many of a charismatic persuasion think that healing is in the oil. Please, dear saint, look at the context of the passage. The context presupposes *Body relationship:*

- A relationship to elders (overseers of a local assembly where the sick person is in communion/fellowship and in submission to its government—James 5:14)

- A submission to their scrutiny over one's life (James 5:15b)

- A scrutiny to inspect for sin (James 5:15b-16)

As the result of submitting to the scrutiny of spiritual oversight, the believer is anointed and then the prayer of faith is offered. In the American charismatic church we have excised the anointing and the prayer of faith from its relational and Body dynamic context! It is utterly absurd to believe that an individual saint whose relationship to the Body and overseeing leadership is not right has any sort of spiritual credibility with a squirt of oil (see James 5; 1 Cor. 11)! That individual could pour it out by the gallon and there would be no spiritual substance—just a lot of charismatic froth! The oil is a symbol, a seal, a witness, or testimony that the individual is in right relationship to the Body, there being no breach of the unity of the Spirit. Psalm 133 so clearly relates the anointing oil with unity.

Let me reiterate it simply: ***Our demand for privacy stops the flow of God's miraculous supply.*** No one will overcome a legalistic and demanding performance spirit who has a disdainful, independent, or sep-aratist attitude toward others. God will not do from heaven what He expects His supernaturally filled Body to accomplish for each other, in His strength and grace endowment.

BATTEN DOWN THE HATCHES

"When thou art come in, thou shalt shut the door upon thee and upon thy sons" (2 Kings 4:4).

The prophet's admonition to the widow is this: Bring the things that are at risk from the creditor (in this case, her sons) into the place of privacy. I believe this speaks of the importance of prayer: the prayer closet.[12] Matthew 6:6 speaks of prayer in almost the same words. We can never overlook or underestimate the importance of prayer in overcoming a legalistic spirit. However, prayer itself can become a religious and legal bondage that is self-defeating. The point of prayer is not necessarily that we get an immediate "answer" for our legal bondage. Add prayer, get deliverance—it is a misconception.

God will often frustrate our prayer, make it very unenjoyable, seemingly unfruitful and unanswered, to teach us the very real lesson that the point of prayer is not getting an answer, but touching Him. I am convinced there will be no freedom from a legalistic spirit until an individual has received an experiential touch and revelation of Calvary grace. That usually comes through prayer *and* crisis, not just prayer. God provides the crisis. We provide the prayer.

Elisha was looking for a specific response, a specific obedience, but it was not duty obedience. It was faith obedience. Prayer and obedience to what you hear are necessary in order to receive the miracle you want. Elisha did not tell the widow to deal with the creditor, but to deal with her own faith. Sometimes we want to do spiritual warfare with the devil or whatever "spirit" we think might be oppressing us. Frequently, God is not calling us to that exercise, but rather He wants us to come to grips with our own faith. It is faith that overcomes, not spiritual warfare (see 1 John 5:4). You cannot overcome the law by dealing with law. You overcome it by the hearing of faith.

INTO THE FUTURE

The widow's future was also at stake because of the creditor's demands. To understand this better, we need to discuss the cultural significance of children for an Israelite woman.

The Hebrew/Semitic culture and mindset was generational. The widow's generational destiny and future was bound up in her sons. The continuance of the family name was bound up in her sons. The hope of giving birth to a son who might be the Messiah was also deeply ingrained in the psyche of every Jewish parent. To lose one's sons was to have one's future literally taken. Without sons to care for her, a widow in those times (if she remained unmarried) would undoubtedly have been reduced to begging or prostitution if not taken in by a relative. There was no social service relief agency.

In an agrarian culture and economy of subsistence, having an extra relative to support was not like having an aunt move into our spare room. Most peasant families absolutely could not support an additional mouth. The removal of the widow's sons was not just a psychological trauma. As an individual, without her sons, she would have no future.

Indebtedness, by definition, is associated with an action in the past. I owe today for spending what I didn't have yesterday. Legalism, by focusing on the past track record of success and failure, neutralizes our present and robs our future. Legalism cannot accommodate the grace of God that does not relate to or correlate with the merit of my past performance. Legalism takes the believer's hope of a future because it presumes upon God's predicted response based upon past performance. In an instant, in a divine moment of contact with the gracious Spirit of Christ, my past becomes an utter irrelevancy and the creditor's reminder of my debt is nothing more than the voice of the accuser demanding moral payment, which I learn to summarily ignore.

YOU'VE GOT TO BE KIDDING ME!

In Second Kings 4:4, Elisha puts another faith demand on the widow. How frustrating! We are well into this story and still no miracle from the "big man"—nothing but the requirement of faith to act on what is not seen and not possessed. Elisha tells the widow to pour out the little bit that she has into her neighbors' vessels.

It looks so stupid to be gathering empty vessels and trying to fill them with what is obviously inadequate, when you are about to lose your sons! The widow could have said, anywhere in this process, "What has this ridiculous spiritual exercise got to do with saving my sons! Why don't you *do* something?!" Of course, because of the relational trust she and her husband had established with Elisha, she acted in faith on the prophet's word.

We must obey God in the arena He requires of us and He will move in the area of our need. Very often God is after obedience in an area that seems irrelevant to us. This is excruciatingly crucifying to the religious perfectionist who thinks Kingdom progress is achieved through the careful management of one's Christian life rather than the process of death and resurrection.

For example, we might be seeking God and asking Him to deliver us from a judgmental and critical spirit. He speaks back to us: "I want you to regularly invite someone to your house after church services." We respond, "But Lord, what has that go to do with my need?" God's response? Silence. Until we obey on the point He is asking, we do not get additional revelation or understanding on the point of our concern. We can beat down heaven's doors with prayer and fasting and all we will get from heaven is annoying silence. On the contrary, if we respond on the point *He* is targeting, the issue we may be targeting gets addressed.

We must also learn to give out of our own need and lack, not just financially but spiritually. It is not too much of a stretch to say that the oil represents the anointing, the resources of the Holy Spirit. Just as Job was delivered when he prayed for his friends, so the widow's miracle and deliverance came when she poured out what she had into others.

Our deliverance from a legalistic and demanding spirit is quickened when we engage ourselves in the lives of others—decentralizing ourselves. He who loves his life will lose it; he who loses his life will find it.

I once asked my congregation if they wanted me to be a good pastor. Of course all responded with a hearty amen. I then said, "Good. I hereby determine to give you one percent of my attention, time, energy, and emotional resources." It got quiet. Luke 15 says that the good shepherd leaves the 99 for the 1 who is lost. This is not talking about the pastor chasing the disgruntled members of the church trying to keep them happy. The context is self-interpreting. It is talking about sinners who are outside the fold (see Luke 15:7). The good shepherd gives attention to the 1 outside the fold more than the 99 already in. However, emphasizing that is a good way to get fired from many churches. In spite of our all our pretensions of being on the cutting edge and so on, I am convinced that we are, on the whole, a very self-absorbed people. We are the Bob Wileys of the Kingdom—gimme, gimme, I need, I need.[13]

A self-absorbed community is a sitting duck for a spirit of legalism. If we are not engaged outwardly, spending our energies for others, we will spend our energies inwardly. People who are living the Gospel are too exhausted to cause problems in the church. Folks who are others-consumed have neither the time, energy, nor will to engage in internal squabbles and strife. Without the outward focus, a congregation will inevitably embrace a legalistic spirit of faultfinding, criticism, and judgmentalism. Self-preservation will kill supernatural supply.

We must minister out of our lack, step out on what we don't have, get out of the realm of our feelings. It isn't our supply anyway. It is His. Will we act in faith on what He has said?

Many of us might say, "God, You've got to be kidding me! I'm the one in need and I can't even hang on to the little bit I have?"

To which God replies, "Right—spend it for others and I will deliver you."

IT'S YOUR MIRACLE

Only after the widow exercises all the phases of obedient faith does supernatural provision occur. The vessels were filled in the measure of her faith. She got as much as she put herself out for in a season when she could not see anything. The time to exercise faith is not when the oil is flowing, but when we see nothing! In fact, it is the time of obedient faith in darkness and nothingness that determines our capacity to receive when the breakthrough supernatural moment happens.

The widow received as much as she made provision for. We must have large expectancy in God. We are often saints of the shriveled soul. We must have expectancy based on God's ability to provide, not the severity of our situation. The thing about large expectancy is that we frequently have to deal with the emotional trauma of always feeling vacant. It is easy to feel full if one's expectancy is small. The fact that we might feel so empty may be because our capacity for God is large. God must create capacity in order to fill us.

In a sense, Elisha has not been on the scene at all. He has not provided a miracle for her. He led her into her own miracle! She has just been acting in faith on what he said to do. This is an example of the power inherent in a prophet's word when obedient faith is mixed with it. In a sense, it is her miracle, not Elisha's. Her obedient faith released the miracle, not Elisha's wonder-working power. This is an example of a true minister: not looking for a forum to show off their anointing, but an opportunity to point someone else to what is available in them, through the indwelling Spirit of Christ.

CONCLUSION

In our story, the widow is exhorted to sell the oil to pay her debt and to live off of what is left over (see 2 Kings 4:7). Her confession to the man of God of what had just happened releases to her abundance at the word of the prophet. Not only is God's provision designed to meet the need, but to have excess.

We need to learn to live in redemption's overflow. Our glorious salvation did more than cancel our debt to the creditor. He did not bring us from debt to zero. We have not been brought from disfavor to neutral—the striving legalistic mindset of so many believers. We have an infinite credit in Christ. A salvation that only brings us to moral zero, moral neutrality, is insufficient. We will all be back in the red in no time. No, we are forever free from the creditor. The state of the New Covenant believer is one of the abundant life, an eternal credit.

We can readily relate to the doctrines of substitution, atonement, repentance, and pardon because they deal with guilt and penalty. We know all about our moral shortcomings—our I.O.U. to God. We thank God for atonement for our sin. However, a High Priest who brings us into God's presence and keeps us in loving communion with Him in an eternal state of infinite blessedness is more difficult to understand. The former brings us to zero; the latter gives us credit. The blood sprinkled on earth purges sin. The sprinkling in heaven draws us near. Not only are we "in Christ" on the cross and humiliation, we are seated with Him in the heavenlies and exaltation. His glory as the resurrected Son of Man is ours. He shares it with us (see John 17:22). We are not moral debtors on spiritual probation, trying to earn enough credit to have our death sentence commuted. We are pardoned, not paroled. Our sentence has been done away with.

The spiritual ledger of accounts due reads "paid in full" beside my name. Oh, glory be to His wonderful name. I am free, free, free!

We need not fear the creditor's knock.

End Notes

1. "Handwriting of ordinances" (Col. 2:14)—I recommend reading a good commentary to catch the full significance of this verse.

2. Elisha oversaw the school of the prophets. It is likely that the widow's husband was a member of that school.

3. First Peter is an example.

4. Psalm 138:2 refers to God's word being exalted above his name. We must understand this is not referring to "the Bible" as we have come to know it. Nor are we to take this verse as if God's word is some abstraction or commodity that is higher than His Person to whom He must submit, as if the word existed apart from His Person. His word and His name reflect the one same Person and His honor. The Scripture is referring to the highest exalted position of His promises above the other wonderful attributes of His name, emphasizing the honor given to His promises. The comments of John Gill in his *Exposition of the Entire Bible* are herein provided for reference:

   ...but rather it is to be understood of God's word of promise, and his faithfulness in fulfilling it; which, though not a greater attribute than any other, yet is made more known and more illustrious than the rest; and particularly may regard the promise of the coming of the Messiah, and of the blessings of grace by him; Jarchi interprets it particularly of the pardon of sin. It may with propriety be applied to Christ, the essential Word, that was made flesh, and dwelt among men; whom God has highly exalted, and not only given him a name above every name of men on earth, but also above any particular name or attribute of his: or however he has magnified him "according" to every name of his, it being his will that men should honor the Son as they honor the Father; or "with" every name along with each of them; or "besides" every name; for all these senses the word will bear. Some render them, as Ben Melech, "thou hast magnified above all things thy name" and "thy word"; or, as others, "thy name [by] thy word"; see Psalm 8:1; The Targum is, "the words of thy praise above all thy name;" or "over all thy name": everything by which he has made himself known in creation and providence; "thou hast magnified thy word," all being done according to the word said in himself, his decrees and purposes; or declared in his word and promises, whereby he has glorified it.

5. I do not believe the Holy Spirit puts sickness on believers to "teach us a lesson" of some sort. Jesus never used sickness as a teaching method during His earthly ministry and He has not changed His methodology in resurrection. He *removed* the burdens of sickness everywhere He went. Rather, when we find ourselves in sickness as a result of being a member of a fallen race, in a fallen world, there are lessons we can learn that we could not learn any other way. One of those lessons is to experience His wonderful delivering and healing power as well as His grace to persevere through. If I am never in need physically, my doctrine of healing is just pious Christian philosophy. Let our bodies be touched, let us pass through a valley of bodily affliction and it is amazing how much sympathy we develop toward others in their pain and how passionate we can become to pursue the

manifestation of the grace of healing in our communities of faith.

6. Jesus sent them out "two by two"; testimony was confirmed in the mouth of "two or three witnesses."

7. Lennon and McCartney, *Help*, Capitol Records, copyright 1965.

8. J. Konrad Hölé, *You Were Born a Champion, Don't Die a Loser* (Minneapolis: World Press, 1999).

9. Hölé, *You Were Born*.

10. Juanita Bynum, unknown source.

11. John Kingsley Alley, *The Apostolic Revelation* (Rockhampton: Peace Publishing, 2002). I could not disagree more strongly with the author's major premise.

12. See Matthew 6:6—"closet," the secret room, the inner chamber.

13. A character from the movie entitled *What About Bob?* © Touchstone Home Video.

Who Are You?

The Gospel of John is sometimes characterized as the "love" Gospel. Accuracy can suffer inversely to generalization. It is beyond the scope of this writing to go into detail, but the bulk of John's Gospel is a prolonged interpersonal conflict between Jesus and various disputants. From John 3 (perhaps even John 1) through John 10, Jesus is sorely in need of a PR consultant. He does not seem to know the "seven keys to growing a dynamic ministry!" He clearly has not studied His demographics nor His target market. He is pointedly insensitive to seekers, seemingly determined to offend just about everybody. Why, He didn't even offer a staffed nursery! Perhaps He missed the latest church growth seminar in Nazareth or could not afford the registration fee.

Everything He says seems to aggravate somebody: the more religious and legalistic the individual or group, the greater the aggravation, and the more hostile the response. His church gets smaller with the turning of every page. The conflict peaks in John 8 in a whole-hog, "in your face," finger-pointing, insult-hurling, name-calling match.[1] This passage is one of the clearest Scriptural examples of the Mediterranean/Semitic custom of challenge and riposte—the cultural practice of verbal jousting, "one-upmanship" that determines honor status in the community.[2] Our Western sensibilities of propriety—what is considered rude or polite—simply do not apply to the Scriptures. Our cultural concepts of "Gentle Jesus, meek and mild," will not fit John 8.

THAT'LL GET YOU KILLED!

John chapters 7–8 are a microcosm of the cosmic conflict of the Gospel. It is a battle for identity. Who has the right to claim filial relationship with God the Father? Who are sons and who are slaves? Later,

Paul picks up the gauntlet in Galatians chapters 3 and 4 (which we will discuss in another chapter). The battle of the ages is an *identity* and *slavery* dispute.

Jesus had the nerve to tell the literal descendants of Abraham that they were slaves. Yahweh was not their Father! (See John 8:33, 39.) This wonderful "message of God's love" was nearly His last! In John 7:31, many of the Jews believed on Him. In John 8:59, the *same people* want to *kill* Him—from believers to would-be murderers, from hero to zero in their eyes in one chapter. What could cause such a dramatic reversal of affections? *A message about identity.* He asserted His, and challenged theirs.

Nothing stirs religious passions to hatred and murder like preaching a message of freedom to people who think they are already free. Performing religionists do not appreciate being told that God is not impressed with Adamic spiritual gymnastics done in the name of Jesus. God will not stand and applaud the somersaults of the Adamic nature trying to please Him. Exposing the deluded confidence of the privileged always gets you stoned. People do not use granite anymore—wagging tongues and feet hustling through the back exit door are the stones of choice for Americans.

Our churches are full of the bound who think themselves free because somewhere in their misty past they were psychologically strongarmed into muttering a prayer of faith. More concerned about being "nice" than preaching the truth, numb to the Holy Spirit, indifferent to conviction, valuing size over substance and potluck dinners over the presence of God, our churches are full of the walking dead who would not accept Jesus in their pulpits if He walked in and announced Himself on Sunday morning. The prophetic voice of freedom is received as warmly in our day as it was in Moses' and Jesus'.

A SECRET IDENTITY

Knowing our new nature, our identity in Christ, is paramount in overcoming a legalistic and performance-based spirit. In three of the most critical moments in our Lord's life—at His baptism in preparation for the wilderness, on the Mount of Transfiguration preparing for the cross, and on the eve of His crucifixion in John 12—an audible voice from heaven was heard. In each case it affirmed His identity and status as a Son. Jesus did not begin His "work" for the Father (His ministry) until He was first affirmed in His identity as a beloved Son.

We need the same experiential assurance before we launch into service for the Lord. Without the assurance of sonship in our hearts, we will be little more than slaves—insecure production units of the Kingdom. Believers who do not know their God-given identity in Christ—the track their divine train runs on—will be vulnerable to a striving legalistic spirit. They will exhaust themselves trying to be something they are not, doing things for which they are not divinely suited. Discouragement, frustration, and exhaustion will result.

The reason an eagle flies and a fish swims is because their identity suits their environment and mission. An eagle in the water or a fish in the air is a problem. Swimming is only a challenge if you are not suited for the water. Scales and fins are an indication that you are called to swim. In Christ, we are fully equipped for both this life and the next. Knowing one's identity in Christ and knowing Christ within as the source of one's life is the rest we are to labor for. It is the rest promised to the faith-filled sons of the covenant that frees them from a striving and performing spirit. We are sons, not slaves.[3]

SPIRITUAL DOMESTICS: HOUSE SLAVES

The subtleness of a legalistic slavery spirit can be seen in the story of Joshua and the children of Israel in the interaction with the Gibeonites. Just like the account of Tobiah in Nehemiah 13, this story demonstrates how a slavery spirit works its way into the covenant community of faith under false pretense.

Israel had crossed the Jordan, taken Jericho and Ai, and was camped at Gilgal (see Josh. 6–9). The blessings and curses of the covenant with Yahweh had been confirmed at Mount Ebal and Mount Gerazim. Having heard of Joshua's victories at Jericho and Ai, the Gibeonites astutely perceived that they would be next on the "A" list for extermination. So, they disguised themselves and deceived Joshua and Israel by sharing a meal and making a covenantal league with them. (Breaking of bread or sharing a meal was a covenantal act in ancient culture, binding each party to mutual protection.)

When Joshua discovered that the Gibeonites had deceived him, he realized that Israel could not destroy them because of the covenant so recently ratified. Even though the covenant was made deceitfully, its terms were still binding. (For ancient people, the ethos of covenant took precedence over even truth and falsehood.) Therefore, instead of executing the Gibeonites, Joshua put them under a curse and made them "slaves of the sanctuary." They became responsible for the most menial tasks of service in the house of God: hauling wood and drawing water for the operation and maintenance of the altar of God.

The result of this covenant had two sides. For Israel, it meant they were forever in league with a people who did not share their covenantal heritage with Yahweh. For the Gibeonites it meant they were bound to slavery in the house of the Lord. Jewish history says the Gibeonites became the Nethinim, the non-Levitical tabernacle servants nearly wiped out by Saul in Second Samuel 21:1-6. David replaced their ministry when he instituted his new order of Davidic worship (see Ezra 8:20).

The Gibeonites could labor for Israel and Yahweh, but they could never inherit the promise made to the covenant sons of Abraham. They were slaves in the midst of a nation of sons. The Gibeonite spirit of slavery in the midst of the sanctuary has present-day church application.

HOP ON BOARD

The Gibeonites responded to God out of fear of destruction at the hand of Joshua. They had heard of his fame and wanted to save their own necks. Sometimes people join a local assembly because of the bandwagon effect. A local church that is experiencing a measure of "success" as defined by our culture (i.e. numbers and money) will draw folks who want to join the ministry for the wrong reasons: *"Why don't we try The First Church of What's Happening Now End-Time Apostolic Ministry and World Outreach Training Center down the road? I hear great things are going on. All our children's friends attend there. Why don't we make a change for the children's sake? They have a great program for the youth. The nursery is great. The parking lot is paved. I hear they are really cutting-edge. I think God is leading us to make a change."*

The question of covenant commitment to the present local assembly doesn't even figure into the thought process. For some, it is all about "services rendered" by the fellowship—a self-centered consumerist mindset. The motive for belonging is not the result of divine planting. It is about what the fellowship offers them. Like the Gibeonites, it is all about self-interest and self-preservation. Adapting and applying President

Kennedy's memorable phrase would slow down the bandwagon: Ask not what your church can do for you, but what you can do for your church.

Without a dramatic divine encounter, such individuals will never be long-term building material in the new fellowship. They will always be slaves. They will produce because they have to, because they have learned the Christian system, but they will never have the heart of the pastor. When the new fellowship ceases to "meet their needs" in some way or the other, they will simply change to another church that does a better job of pandering to unbridled self-interest masquerading as "being led by God."

It takes no courage or faith to join something that is already a success. It takes great faith and stamina to stick with something to make it a success. The rotating sheep syndrome in America is a scandal— professional cross-dodgers who rotate from church to church wanting to receive "the latest," rather than be a living sacrifice. They are psychologically thin-skinned people whose mission in life seems to be finding an offense anywhere they can and drifting from church to church trying to catch the latest wave of what God is doing. When the tide goes out, so do they—to the next church.

LOOK AT ME! I AM SOMEBODY!

The Gibeonites also desired to make league with Joshua because of matters of fame and reputation. They appealed with flattery to Joshua's sense of reputation. They wanted to hook up with the winning team without sharing the sacrifice and burden of what makes the team a winning one. There is a lot of pressure for folks to link up because of fame and reputation of the ministry or the minister. Because of a psychological maladjustment, they will gladly embrace slavery in a performance-based system in exchange for a personal sense of identity, albeit a false one. They feel good because they are associated with the biggest church in town, the most famous minister, or whatever.

Having no inner identity of their own from a revelation of the abiding Spirit of Christ, individuals seek to get name recognition from joining something "successful" in their community. Those who belong to a church because of the affirmation and fame that comes from being successful will be the first to jump ship if the reason for the fame and acclaim passes. Fame exists only as long as clients receive some emotional, psychological, or physical benefit. Should the church fail to provide the service, should the definition of "cool" change, the client withholds the notoriety and fame vanishes—as many one-hit-wonder rock stars have realized.

The devil offers fame. God offers honor. Fame is temporary, dependent notoriety, independent of character. Honor is dependent on character, independent of notoriety.

YOU CAN'T BELIEVE YOUR EYES

Entering into covenant with Canaanites was strictly forbidden (see Exod. 23:32; Deut. 7:2). Relying on sensory evidence rather than spiritual discernment, Joshua made a covenant without a priest and without the shedding of blood. He made a pact with folks in a *false identity*. For the Gibeonites, it was not a bad deal considering the alternative was extinction! For Israel it was certainly not an ideal situation. It would be like having to put up with a chain gang doing your yard work: They do it because they have to, but if they had the chance, they would break and run and stab you in the back on the way.

A performance-based, legalistic, slavery spirit can deceive even the best spiritual leaders because it comes across innocently as volunteerism. The Gibeonites volunteered for slavery! (See Joshua 9:8-9.) Folks will gladly sell themselves to volunteerism just for a chance to have an identity and to relationally belong to something. This is the basis of all the civic good-works associations.[4] Too often the Church of the Lord is little more than a religious fraternity, a good-works association.

Folks with an uncrucified servant gift are the most vulnerable to a false slavery spirit of volunteerism. They want to volunteer for everything out of their identity insecurity. Since most small-to-medium churches are constantly looking for help, these individuals end up *serving* but never really *coming to the cross* to receive death and Kingdom life. These are the folks who can usually be seen buzzing around an assembly in a hustle and bustle—but who are conspicuously absent or disengaged from the more spiritual dynamics of praise, intercession, and worship. They are too busy for that.

The way to help such individuals into spirit and life is to deny them opportunity to serve. Make them stop, sit down, and put someone else less competent than themselves in the task they were doing or want to do. This will purge the motive of the person with the servant's gift and force him or her to go to Calvary—squirming, complaining, and probably gossiping and accusing you all the way!

Why is this important? Servant-slaves, volunteers, will always revolt and turn against sons in a season of crisis. If you do not help a servant-slave touch Calvary, it will be just like having the Gibeonites in your midst.

We have been called to something better. Our covenant has not been made in deceit but in Spirit and Truth. We have been joined into covenant with the Son of God Himself by an act of Christ's shed blood and eternal priesthood. We have been given a new name and a new identity. We do not have to find acceptance with the Greater Joshua (Jesus) by pretending to be something we are not. He accepts us in our damaged identity and gives us a new one.

Revelation speaks of the overcomer having a new name written on him (see Rev. 2:17; 3:12). The new name written on the believer is the new identity in Christ—the new creation being resulting from the union of the Spirit of Christ with an individual human spirit.

WRESTLING WITH A CORPSE

Is it possible for the Adamic nature to obey and satisfy God's requirements? Of course not. Some think that the process of Christian maturity is characterized by trying to subdue and wrestle the Adamic nature into submission. The Adamic nature is *neither trainable nor redeemable*. It is cursed. It is under a death sentence, not a rehab process. Its destiny is the mortuary, not the gym. Since God knows He cannot get obedience out of the Adamic nature, in our conversion and regeneration, He puts the very nature of His Son in us. That nature, the new creation, the spirit man, then becomes the seat of all of God's transactions in me. Any obedience I muster has as its fountainhead the gift of the life of the Son of God freely given to me. Why, then, would God reward me for what He has given me? My obedience is God's gift to me, not my gift to God. I do not obey to earn His blessing. I am blessed so I can obey.

One might ask about the command to put to death the deeds of our flesh (see Rom. 8:13; Col. 3:5). Indeed, we must do that, but it is the source that makes the difference. Adam cannot crucify Adam. The strength of the new man is what enables me to put to death the old man, reckoning myself dead in Adam and alive in God.

We are not little puppy dogs who get a biscuit from our heavenly trainer when we obey and get a swat on the nose when we disobey. We are sons. My sonship is the source of my obedience; obedience is not the source of my sonship.

God does not reward me for my obedience. He rewards faith. God rewards those who believe that He is and who diligently seek Him. Without *faith* it is *impossible* to please Him. It is my faith in Christ and reckoning into the power of His death and resurrection in me that provides access to the benefits of being a covenant son, not how far under par I can maintain myself on the links of life. I do not have to provide Him with my scorecard at the end of each day.

We readily understand that God loved us while we were yet sinners. We grasp that salvation is a free gift—my lifestyle of disobedience having no bearing whatsoever on His blessing me with the gift of salvation in the presence of repentance and faith. However, somehow after I am saved, it is now my obedience that determines if He blesses me or not. Whence cometh the shift?

Jesus said He desires mercy, not sacrifice. A commitment to act better is a sacrifice. God is not impressed by sacrifice anymore. We cannot please God any more than what Jesus has already done. Grace and mercy are received from above freely, not earned by diligent commitment to biblical principles.

SONS OR SLAVES?

To help discern the degree to which someone may be under the influence of a slavery spirit, let's examine some contrasts between slaves and sons.

First, we need to understand the concept of slavery from a 1st century Roman perspective, which is different from the mid-19th century American cultural perspective associated with racism. What did Jesus or Paul have in mind when they thought of slavery?

Slaves composed a large part of the agricultural work force in parts of the Roman Empire (e.g., Italy). They often competed with free peasants for the same work. Slaves were found in all professions and generally had more opportunity for social advancement than free peasants. Unlike the vast majority of slaves in the United States and the Caribbean, they were able to work for and achieve freedom, and some freed slaves became independently wealthy. This social mobility applied especially to the household slaves—the only kind of slave addressed in Paul's writings. Economically, socially, and with regard to freedom to determine their future, these slaves were better off than most free persons in the Roman Empire. Most free persons were rural peasants working as tenant farmers on the vast estates of wealthy landowners.[5]

Simply put, POW's from the various parts of the conquered empire became slaves. It was a matter of power, economics, and conquest—not race.

GET OUT OF MY HOUSE!

Slaves can be dismissed at any time. It is not possible to be "un-sonned." A son is a son by generation, not performance. Slaves are secure to the degree of their faithful execution of tasks. If they do not faithfully execute a task, the master may get rid of them by dismissing or killing them. A son, by reason of the family name, has a better relationship. He is not dismissed when he does not produce a good or service—*disciplined* because of carnality, *yes*, but dismissed because of unfaithfulness...NO. His privilege and status as a member of the family entitles him to better treatment than a slave.

Countless Christians suffer under the weight of a slavery spirit. Striving to perform in perfect obedience, they hope God will not banish them from the religious plantation. The Scriptures state it summarily: The slave abides not in the house but the son abides forever (see John 8:35). Slaves are never secure in their place in the "house" of God.

PURGING PUNISHMENT

I try to encourage my congregation to take the word "punishment" or "chastisement" out of their vocabulary and substitute it with "child training." The concept of punishment is never used in the New Testament in relationship to sons. Slaves can be punished; sons are child-trained. This is more accurate both theologically and grammatically. The New Testament translates various Greek words into "punished" or "punishment." Together the connotation is "retribution, vindication, chastisement, and penalty." The significant point to know is that they are never used in reference to the believer. There is no retribution and penalty for those who are in Christ Jesus! There is no pending punishment in this life or the next for the sons (and daughters) of the covenant!

Child training (or "chastisement" in the King James Version) is the portion of covenant sons. The Greek word translated as chastisement is *paideía*. It means the whole training and education of children (which relates to the cultivation of mind and morals).[6] It also includes the training and care of the body. Child training can contain a negative element to our flesh, but it is not punishment for failure. The consequences of sin and our own foolish decisions are not child training. They are the result of sowing and reaping, the logical results of what we have done to violate the laws of God's moral universe. Now, God can gloriously redeem our mistakes and wonderfully weave them into the tapestry of our redemptive history, but these self-inflicted sins and blunders are not the same as the determinate training of the Father.

Our own sins and failures take away our hope. God's child training is designed to give us hope and a future. God's training discipline is with design and purpose. Our sins yield destruction. In fact, only sons are capable of receiving the Father's child training. If we should find ourselves under the disciplining hand of God, it is proof that we belong to Him. Child training, not punishment, is the signet of our sonship (see Prov. 3:11-12; Heb. 12:8-11). ***Only when we have received purging of our sins and the full assurance of sonship are we even trainable material!***[7]

A son can be secure under the disciplining and child-training hand of a father. A slave will never be secure. If believers struggle in their inner psychology with nagging doubts of security, a slavery mentality may be a root cause. Slaves are punished for failure. Sons are disciplined to promote growth.

TAPPING INTO IT

Inheritance is one of the greatest themes of both the Old and New Testaments. Slaves may faithfully serve in the house until the day they die, but because they are not heirs, they can go to their grave and never receive an inheritance. It takes more than faithfulness and loyalty to possess an inheritance. A son does not have to perform to merit his inheritance. It is determined by his *relationship* with the testator and the *will* of the testator.

Now, in the Roman civil system it was possible for a slave to be an inheritor through the process of adoption (which we will examine in a later chapter) and a thoroughly profligate son could be disinherited. But it was not possible for a slave to come into an inheritance until he first had the civil status of a son. Slaves had no privileges. They earned everything.

Sons had privileges by reason of birth. In Roman society, when a son came of age, all that was his father's became his.

Don't Give Me an Instruction Manual—Give Me the Key!

I have found that the Church universal often overlooks one of the great dimensions of our faith. It is the key dimension in terms of success in practical living, including overcoming legalism and performance-based religion. We adequately teach on justification, sanctification, glorification, and other themes. Perhaps the average saint might even be able to explain a term or two. However, we are not as proficient in understanding and explaining the doctrine of appropriation. Appropriation is *how* we avail ourselves of what our justification has bought us.

How frustrating and debilitating it would be to tell someone of a great treasure that is his, give him instruction manual after instruction manual that described how wonderful the treasure is and how to unlock the box, *but then never give him the key!* In this scenario, folks would eventually resent being told about the treasure…as well as resent the person who told them about it! Without the *key*, all the treasure in the world is of no practical avail because you cannot get into what is yours! Without the *key*, all the correct instruction about the treasure will actually *produce* a legalistic and slavery spirit. An understanding of the doctrine of appropriation and inheritance is the key that unlocks justification's fruit.

Understanding our privileged status as sons in Christ is vital to overcoming a legalistic and performance-based spirit. My status as a covenantal son means that I have privileged access to all of heaven's resources at my time of need, not just from 11:00 a.m. to 12:30 p.m. on Sundays! I am not disqualified or shunned because of my poor behavior.[8]

Get Away from Me

I am very uncomfortable with a form of child discipline used by many parents in association with a "time out" policy. Many parents will discipline their children in this manner: "I want you to go to your room and stay there until you get control of yourself. Now, when you have regained composure, you can come back out." Think of what this reinforces in a child's mind: *When you sin, you must be removed from my presence as a parent.* In other words, *I do not want you around. Your behavior requires that I physically separate from you.*

The practice will actually reinforce a legalistic spirit in our children. We wonder why, when they become adolescents, they hate us and hate God. If they manage to stumble into a semblance of Christianity, they are afflicted with the baggage of legalistic psychology.

How contrary to the Gospel! When we sin, our privilege and status as sons means we have access to the Father in our time of need! We are not supposed to run away from Him, but *to* Him!

Also, this form of child training (using "time outs") reinforces a performance-based mindset because it is up to the child to fix himself to regain relational access to the parent. Regaining his composure is the "condition" that must be met in order for the child to come out of separation and isolation and be restored to interaction with the parent. What have we done with such thinking? We have told the child that if he wants to be with us he must *earn it*—and earn it *alone*. If he has a weakness, he must fix it, because until he fixes himself he does not have access to my adult presence. Dear reader, we program our children from the earliest ages into a performance-based mindset that is utterly contrary to the grace of God and, in so doing, we are actually undermining the grace of God in their lives.

You might ask, "What should I do?"

I am completely convinced of the superiority of corporal punishment done in a controlled atmosphere—not with anger, rage, or abuse. It forces your child to interact with you personally. Corporal punishment is quick, soon forgotten, and if done correctly, can be used to constrain the child to have personal interaction with you, the parent, both before and after the "moment." This is the way God's Kingdom works. When we constrain our children to interact with us in their weakness and disobedience, accepting discipline, correction, love, and acceptance, we are setting them up to succeed in a Kingdom that operates by grace, love, and relationship—not legalism, performance, isolation, and relational separation.

PASSPORT PLEASE

Roman slaves were separated from family and country. As non-citizens in their new land, they had neither civic identity, nor privileges, nor responsibility. As long as they faithfully executed the "micro" tasks of their master's wishes, they did not have to engage themselves in any of the "macro" responsibilities of citizenship. They experienced the culture they lived in, but they were not responsible for any contribution to that culture. They did not have a shareholder stake in the society. Their feelings toward the culture could be conflicted. On the one hand, it is the culture of their existence; but on the other hand, its demise would not break their heart.

A slavery spirit in the church has similar qualities. Some folks actually prefer the drudgery of task and function to the responsibility of "church citizenship." When someone becomes a citizen they must assume the burdens and responsibilities of citizenship, including defense. When a believer is not a cultural stakeholder it is like they enjoy the privileges of the culture without the responsibility of ownership. Being a citizen, not only of heaven but of a local church assembly, means I do not get to enjoy just the blessings of the covenant community—I am also responsible for the covenant community.

Non-stakeholders want to criticize the leadership and the church assembly for everything that is wrong. When referring to the corporate assembly and its leaders they use the pronouns they and them—the other guys, the leaders, the unenlightened. Stakeholders use we and us, not they and them.

CITIZEN SOLDIERS

The difference between slaves and stakeholders is like the difference between the *pledge* of allegiance and the *oath* of allegiance. Civilians say the *pledge* of allegiance. It is a verbal commitment to ideals and principles. It is a philosophical statement that requires no personal cost or sacrifice. *Others* sacrificed to establish the philosophy that civilians can agree to. Soldiers, on the other hand, take the *oath* of allegiance. The oath is a commitment to defend, unto death, what civilians have agreed to in philosophy.

Citizenship in the Kingdom requires "citizen soldiers," not just civilians. If we want to enjoy the privileges of the covenant community we must take the responsibility of its defense—from enemies without in all forms, and from enemies within such as gossip, slander, criticism, backbiting, judgmentalism, perfectionism, and a host of other in-house infections.

Merely meeting religious expectations as a slave is safer, easier, and less costly than being a personal stakeholder—a citizen soldier in God's Kingdom, expressed in the local covenant community.

NO NAMES AND NEW NAMES

Slaves do not share the family name or image. They experience family life, in a sense, by reason of their presence in the home, but they are not really part of the family. They can faithfully work for their master, but they do not share the family name. The only hope they have is that they might be taken into the family through adoption. That is, if they work hard enough and long enough, they might qualify for adoption into the family.

Sons, on the other hand, are identified at birth. They bear a family name and family image or resemblance. Now, in the course of that child's life, he or she might bring dishonor to both the name and the image, but they do not have to earn either. From the moment of birth, a son has access to all the privileges, blessings, and responsibilities associated with bearing the family name and image. Some of the privileges may have to be "grown up" into, but they are present at the moment of new birth.

SPENT FUEL CELLS

Too many churches emphasize issues of authority and submission rather than mutual love and charismatically endowed service. It is expected that people give themselves for the "vision of the house." In such atmospheres, individuals can end up being treated like expendable commodities. They become the necessary consumable, the fuel, that drives the leader's pursuit of whatever the local dream or vision may be. This climate does not necessarily happen with purpose or malice. But it does happen. When a lump of coal is used up...it is used up. It retains its form, but it is really just a collection of ashes, only bearing a resemblance of what it used to be.

Folks who are more like pack mules for the leader's dreams and ambitions than relational covenant brothers will sooner or later be prone to backsliding, resentment, and severe disenchantment with the local church and the organization. It is not that the dreams and visions in a leader are not birthed of God. *The method of implementation makes all the difference!* Right dream plus wrong method equals performance-based religion and slavery.

I am not opposed to visionary leadership but a few things must be kept in proper perspective:

When passion for vision exceeds love for one another and the world, we are in a Christian cult, not the Lord's Church. Participation in the dream must be completely voluntary. Individuals who do not want to "hop on the train" must not be viewed, consciously or otherwise, as riding in the second-class compartment on the train of the leader's dream. It is not a matter of giving up the dream and vision. It is a matter of having a dream and vision large enough to include those who do not want to make the trip! This is only possible in the revelation of the New Covenant (next chapter).

When focus and emphasis is on fulfilling the great dream rather than loving one another and the world, we have opened the door to a master-slave spirit. Sooner or later, faithful people will be exhausted and perhaps not really know why. Leaders will be frustrated and relational separation and alienation will result. Sooner or later, if given a chance, the slaves will leave—disenchanted, resentful, and hurt. Apostolic and fathering love requires that it be the *leaders* who are spent as consumables for the equipping and dream realization of the congregation. It is about giving our lives away—spending and being spent—so others reach their destiny. My destiny as a leader is to be consumed for Christ's cause in the life of others. It is about helping them reach their destiny, not me being conscious of fulfilling mine (see 2 Cor. 12:15).

SERVILE OBEDIENCE

Slaves live by commands from the master. They can only do what the master tells them to do. They have no independent rights to self-determination or action. They simply must follow the rules. They have to be told everything. Sons, however, live out of love for the father. They know the father's heart by reason of communion and access. Through relationship, sons do not always need specific instruction. Jesus said, "If you abide...ask what you will" (see John 15:7). A heart that is truly won does not require constant divine communication and instruction. Mutual hearts rest in one another's love.[9]

For sons, output is not the basis of their relationship with their father. Rather, relationship is the basis of their service. Production flows not as a result of striving but of abiding. How appropriately the Scriptures link productivity to abiding (see John 15). We think fruitfulness is the result of working hard. That ethic may hold true for a New England Yankee in the realm of commerce, but "God helps those who help themselves" is a saying that has no place in the Kingdom. Abiding is a quality of sonship. Production is a quality of slavery. Service is not a strong enough bond to keep us in covenantal relationship. Only love is the bond of the cement of perfection (maturity).

CONCLUSION

Some might object to this chapter by saying, "Are we not called to be the servants or 'bond slaves' of the Lord?" Often the Scripture uses seemingly contradictory metaphors. Such is the case here of sons and slaves. We simply must not mix the metaphors. Rather, they are heads and tails of the same coin.

In terms of our calling and ministry, yes, we are the bond slaves of the Lord. We have no rights. He bought us out of the slave market— literally, redeemed us—and as such we are His servants. However, in terms of our identity, relationship, and expression of life, we are not slaves. We are sons. I do not serve to gain a sense of identity. Because I have been given a new identity, I serve. I do not obey to gain a sense of acceptance. Because I have been accepted, I obey. I am not rewarded for my obedience. My obedience is my reward. I do not lose His favor when I fail. I am favored in failure so I can be loved into victory. I do not fear His rejection. I reject fear of His rejection. I do not qualify to experience His life. I have experienced His life, which qualifies me to enjoy it. I am not punished when I disobey. I suffer the consequences of unbelief.

I am not a slave. I am a son.

.

End Notes

1. It is very important to pay attention to language and cultural nuances to get the full force of the intensity of the conflict.

2. Refer to Malina and Rohrbaugh, *Social Science Commentary of the Gospel of John*.

3. Throughout this text I will use the term *sons* in a gender-inclusive manner. Daughters are included.

4. Some examples are: Rotary, Elks, Moose, Odd Fellows, Masons, and many others.

5. This paragraph was paraphrased from *IVP Background Commentary: New Testament*, Craig S. Keener, ed. (Downers Grove: Intervarsity Press). Retrieved from: Quick Verse 7.0, CD-ROM (Cedar Rapids: Parsons Technology, 1993). Electronic Edition STEP Files, 1997.

6. Thayer, J.H. *The New Thayer's Greek-English Lexicon*. J.P. Green, Sr., ed. (Peabody: Hendrickson, 1981).

7. See the Book of Hebrews, which shows us that purging precedes assurance, which precedes discipline. The order is *critical!*

8. "Let us therefore come boldly unto the throne of grace" (Heb. 4:16). The word translated "boldly" is the Greek word *parrhesia*, meaning complete freedom of speech, candor, "telling it like it is, without hesitation, concealment, vagueness, fearless confidence, and assurance."

9. I really get nervous around folks who proclaim to have this open, ongoing dialogue with God as if the Almighty had nothing better to do than maintain a personal dialogue with the individual. Some folks think they are somehow more mature or more spiritual if they have a constant patter of divine instruction going in and out of their spirits: God told me this, and God told me that, etc. Divine radio chatter is not the sign of spirituality or maturity. The abundance of personal divine communication may be more indicative of one's immaturity and slave spirit. Slaves have to be constantly instructed. Fathers and sons rest in one another's love and mutuality of will. Abundance of allegedly heavenly communication just might mean that you are a self-centered infant who needs constant attention.

The New Covenant Life

Like many ministers, Paul passed through seasons where finances did not exactly abound. However, there was one thing Paul had in regular abundance: critics. Even his preacher friends couldn't understand him half the time (see 2 Pet. 3:15-16). He was undermined, misrepresented, abandoned, rejected, despised, and lied about. So much for his friends. Numerous opponents from within and without the church distorted Paul's message, turning the grace of God into a religious scheme that justified licentiousness and lasciviousness (see Rom. 6:1; Jude 4). Misunderstandings and misrepresentations are only two of the delightful fringe benefits of the call to preach.

A friend of mine once gave me some advice that, at first blush, seemed a little extreme, but I think actually captured a fundamental reality: "If you are not accused of promoting a casual lifestyle, you are probably not preaching apostolic grace." Folks who emphasize the "high standard" are frequently the most difficult to awaken to the depths of biblical grace. They are likely to accuse those who emphasize grace as having a "low standard."

A pastor friend of mine once confessed (quite happily and passionately) that his articulated goal in ministry was to keep his congregation in perpetual fear every Sunday, lest they should fall into casual living. He pastored a very "successful" mainline evangelical church.

Another friend of mine, a good man who oversees a network of scores of churches, confided in me that in all his years of Christian experience neither he nor anyone else in his network had ever received solid, systematic, exegetical, and doctrinal instruction about the New Covenant! The brother had many great insights from Old Testament typology and various topical matters of Christendom. His character was impeccable. But concerning the *key* element of what makes us Christians, he was utterly in the dark! Is it any wonder that performance-based religion is so prevalent in the Church as to practically be considered the norm? This man was an *apostolic leader*, responsible for influencing hundreds if not thousands of lives. Although his honesty and candor speaks to his transparent integrity, it belies a staggering need.

Casual living *can* result from a doctrine of radical grace, but it does not *have to*. If my choice is between two evils, I choose the risk of casual living over the suffocating fear and bondage of performance-based religion. Fortunately, we do not have to settle for either option. In earlier chapters I briefly touched on issues of obedience, holiness, and legalism. It is time to evaluate the matter in detail.

FALSE FREEDOM

Theologians have a term for the abuse of the doctrine of grace: antinomianism. It applies particularly to the somewhat unfair logical extension and distortion of John Calvin's doctrine of election and irresistible grace. The term is a compound word from the Greek words *anti*, meaning "instead of" or "against"; *nomos*, meaning "law" (or "the law"); and *ism*, meaning "belief system." We need to be careful in using the term "law." Sometimes in Scripture it applies specifically to the Mosaic code and at other times it is broader, meaning any moral or ethical system.

The "CliffsNotes" summary of the logic of antinomianism is this: Since I am elected to salvation, predetermined by the Lord, and under grace for past, present, and future sins, my disobedience cannot undo God's election. God no longer holds me accountable to obedience. I cannot obey unless His grace enables me. Since it is all up to His grace, my obedience (or lack thereof) is really His problem. If I fail Him, it is because He just hasn't given me enough grace. Since I am unconditionally chosen in Him and eternally secure, I don't need to worry about it.

Allowing for some editorializing, this is not too much of a caricature. Thousands of folks believe this, or some variation of it. They think the rest of us live an incomplete and immature form of Christianity if we are concerned about obedience at all.

I personally know a pastor who began to embrace this view. He believed the Church universal had a deficient view of the depth of God's grace. In his mind he had discovered "lost truth" concerning grace. He began to practice his liberty with alcohol and tobacco[1] and ended up in fornication and divorce, all without a shred of conviction because he was "under grace." Well, dear reader, if you have read this book thus far and think I am endorsing a form of hyper-spiritual antinomianism, this is my chance to set you at ease. The *genuine* grace of God received by the *genuinely* born again is a *teaching* and *sanctifying* grace:

> *For the grace of God that bringeth salvation hath appeared to all men [humanity], teaching us that, denying ungodliness and worldly lusts, we should live soberly, righteously, and godly, in this present world* (Titus 2:11-12).

The same grace of God that brings salvation produces obedience and holiness. A message of grace that does not result in obedience and holiness is not biblical grace, but a sound-alike counterfeit. Obedience-less grace is no grace at all. *However*, obedience is the fruit of grace, not the root of grace. This distinction and order must be maintained. The questions that need to be asked are not whether or not obedience is required, but *what is the source* of our obedience and *how is it realized?*

Consider a garden hose lying in the sun in July. If you should take a drink out of the end of the hose, the first few sips would be warm and taste like hose! However, the more the water flows, the cooler it becomes and the less it tastes like hose! That is the way of New Covenant obedience. It is not a matter of focusing on the "hose-iness" of my old nature and trying to get it to taste better. It never will. The issue is the release of the flow of the life that has been given me in Christ. As the water of life flows, it has its own purgative effect. The more flow of the indwelling life there is in me, the less of the taste of Adam will I have. The flow of the life within is released as I embrace death and resurrection. Life begets holiness. Holiness does not beget life.

SOURCE TOXICITY

Suppose a farmer unknowingly planted his entire orchard in soil that drew its water from a contaminated source. The trees then grew, in a limited, sick, and deficient way, but never produced any fruit. No amount of fertilizer or care caused the orchard to produce. Upon discovery of the toxic source, the farmer immediately uprooted the orchard and replanted it in good soil, its root system drawing from a healthy source of water. Instantly and effortlessly the trees returned to health and bore fruit in due season without any strain. The lesson? *Connect the tree with a good source, and it will inevitably bear fruit.* The tree (the seed) has within it the inherent power to bring forth fruit.

It is the same in the Kingdom. Many leaders and saints are working hard, fertilizing their Adamic tree with God's Word, pruning with biblical disciplines of prayer and fasting, only to be disappointed that the life they were given to believe was theirs, the abundant life, full of glory, is an illusion. Instead, they experience the arid life of dogma, personal projections, and expectations of others, and the drudgery associated with trying to "produce" Christianity. Treating the Adamic tree kindly will never produce godly fruit. Even with godly fertilizer (God's Word) the tree will never bear. It cannot. Its source is utterly contaminated.

Knowing the Adamic nature was hopelessly contaminated, yet still requiring holiness from His creation, God took the matter in His own hands. He made a covenant with Himself and put His own nature into humanity (see Heb. 6:13-20; Gen. 15; Pss. 2, 110; Ezek. 36; Jer. 31, 33). His own Spirit, His nature, His seed in us becomes the source of the obedience He requires (see 1 Pet. 1:23; 2 Pet. 1:4).

The key to obedience in a believer's life is an awakening to a new life source and the means of releasing its power. This brings us to God's ultimate remedy for legalistic and performance-based religion: the gift of the indwelling Spirit in New Covenant, and His life released through His cross.

It's Not My Life, Man

The New Covenant is not merely a change in *power* rating, like switching from a 50- to 100-watt bulb. A change in bulbs results in more output, but the source is the same. The New Covenant is a change in *life source*, a new center of consciousness and being. The difference is like changing from a horse-drawn buggy to an automobile. The very life source of the power has changed to a new order. In the New Covenant, the source of obedience has changed from man's soul life to the indwelling Spirit of Christ. God has given us a new fountainhead of life within.[2]

Grandpa's Pump

Most who read this are likely too young to remember the days of pre-indoor plumbing. In rural prairie Canada in the 1960s, my grandparents still had an outhouse and a hand pump in the yard.[3] Imagine if the pump was tapped into a contaminated well. You could work the handle for hours and all you are going to get is bad water. You could memorize the pump manual, practice pumping, and spend all day at it. You are not going to get what you want because *the source is contaminated*. If you want to get better water, the pump has to be *relocated* to a *new source*. Once tapped into a clear source, there would be no problem getting good water.

Grandpa's pump is like humanity's condition. God does expect obedience. The problem is that the source in Adam is utterly contaminated. It will never produce God's holiness. Most Christians live their lives trying hard, frantically pumping on a contaminated source, thinking that by much activity and effort they can produce the obedience God requires. It is a futile endeavor. Humanity needs a source change.

The only way an observer could tell if the pump was bringing good water or not would be to taste it. If the source was contaminated, it might take hours, days, months, or years to manifest a medical problem, depending on the nature of the contaminate.

This is what makes legalism and performance-based religion so subtle. You cannot tell by observation who is a genuine believer and who is not. The outward exertion looks the same. New Covenant obedience is a *source* matter not an *effort* matter—change the source, get the life.

Once we are tapped into the new source, obedient life results. The new birth has inherent power to manifest itself in holiness. I do not believe in powerless, creedal, confessional conversions. A converted life is an empowered life. I am not endorsing instantaneous freedom from every sin and besetting weaknesses. But I am advocating for a great God who would not require of His new creation that which He has not supplied resource to accomplish.

BROTHER "PUMPS-A-LOT"

The life we have been given in Him is like an artesian well. We do not have to flail the Adamic pump handle trying to make Christianity happen. It cannot be coerced to manifest through the application of biblical principles. If yielded to through the process of experiential death and resurrection, it flows. The problem is, Adam would rather flail than die. Professional pump-men earn the respect and admiration of others in the Christian community: "Look at how hard Brother Pumps-a-Lot is working for Jesus. Look at his earnestness! Wouldn't it be wonderful if everyone was as devoted as Brother Pumps-a-Lot?"

There is just a small problem. Brother Pumps-a-Lot is not born again. You cannot tell by his activity what kind of water he is bringing up. Religious activity in the name of Jesus is not the same as having a life source change. Adam in a tuxedo with clean fingernails or Adam in begrimed rags is still Adam.

No sir, Adam would prefer to pump in the noonday sun until the sweat is rolling off his nose like water over Victoria Falls than to embrace the death sentence he has in Jesus, yield to the Spirit of Christ within, experience unspeakable deaths, and be brought up again in His life. Adam will always choose the pump handle over the grave.

Bad Code

Some folks approach the New Covenant like a substitute legal system. "We had the 'bad' Old Covenant of Mosaic rules and ordinances, and now we have the 'good' New Covenant made up of better rules and ordinances." This is both simplistic and incorrect. Christian conversion is not a change in operating philosophy. It is not like we have an inner political administration that needs to be replaced as a result of a new election: We choose Jesus! Out with the bad guys! In with the good guys! It is about one nature dying and a new nature being born. One can embrace a new operational philosophy of life that is Christian in its ethics yet never be converted. Grace can be administered legally! The New Covenant is not a substitute legal system, a new code for an old one.

A Ticket to Ride or a Life to Live?

God's plan from the beginning of creation was to have an expression of Himself in time and space—a created image that could reflect His essential nature. In humanity (before the fall) He had created for Himself an associate on the same plane as Himself, a finite being who had capacity for the divine. His expectation was, and is, that His creation would reflect His nature— this includes obedience to the revealed divine will: "Be ye holy as I am holy."

The New Covenant is a covenant of spiritual discernment (knowledge of God), divine fellowship, and moral cleansing. This is the order given in Jeremiah 31. We sometimes want to make moral cleansing the condition for divine fellowship. This reverses God's New Covenant order and is like asking a child to clean himself up before he takes a bath. The bath experience results in cleansing. Moral cleansing is a result of the New Covenant, not the condition of the New Covenant.

As a result of the fall, humanity no longer loves or trusts God. The great work of God is to get humanity to believe in and trust Him. Jesus did not die to give us the "Answers to Life's Questions" book (the Bible) or to get us to heaven. He died to restore us relationally to the Father who is in heaven. What good is it to physically occupy heaven for all eternity if you do not love and trust the One you are with? God's purpose in the New Covenant isn't getting His people's ticket punched for the midnight heavenly express.[4] His purpose is to make a people *relationally His* and establish them in:

- His cleansing

- His ways

- His rest

- His love

- His life

- The knowledge of God

PERSON BEFORE PRINCIPLE

The problem with law and law living is that it never works. Paul makes it clear that the law was just and good, but it was weak in that it depended upon responsiveness in man (see Rom. 7). Because of this weakness, God never intended for law, code, or principle to precede or supercede relationship with Him. This was true even in the Old Covenant era.

The order of events in Exodus 19 and 20 are significant. Israel was to be a covenant nation of kings and priest unto God *first* (see Exod. 19), and then they received the law (see Exod. 20). It was exactly at this point that Israel failed. Rather than engage God in His Personhood, they told Moses to mediate for them and they promised to do everything Moses told them to do.

Israel failed at the point of living relationship, choosing to hear secondhand precepts rather than engaging an awesome, even dreadful, God. They were so deceived that they contradict themselves in the account in Deuteronomy 5:24-25. Even though Moses stands before them as living proof that God talks with man and he lives; they still confess that if they hear His voice they will die. They commission Moses to be their intermediary God-broker, and the rest, as they say, is tragic history. Secondhand revelation and code will never produce a nation of obedient kings and priests.

Israel's relational calling *preceded* their obligation to holy living. So does ours. God's order is never that of revealing Himself to humanity through law and principle. His order is always that of revealing Himself to a person, from which impartation of life and obedience follows. Human personality demands God.

The way of requirement (law) and promise is cursed (see Gal. 3:10). In all the New Testament there is not a single verse encouraging the New Covenant believer to promise to do better, make a covenant with God, make an oath, make a commitment, or the like. In fact, the Scripture says *not* to make any such promise but to let our "yea be yea and nay be nay"— anything more than that is sin. All our vows and resolutions end in denial because we have no power to carry them out.[5]

Christ has redeemed us from "requirement-promise" theology and living—the curse of performance-based religion: God asks, and I promise, I swear, I will do it. That is called an oath, an oath we cannot keep. Colossians 2:14-15 reads:

> *Blotting out the handwriting of ordinances that was against us, which was contrary to us, and took it out of the way, nailing it to His cross; and having spoiled principalities and powers, He made a show of them openly, triumphing over them in it.*

What was the handwriting of ordinances? They were our promise to God to live by rules and principles. You might say that you didn't sign anything. Yes, you and I did. We signed in Adam. We re-sign every time we try to live for God out of performance rather than relationship.

Christ just didn't take the "Mosaic Law" and tack it to the tree. What He took was our signed covenant agreement. But the glorious Gospel is this: The very deal that we signed on to, Jesus Christ has taken and removed. He has taken our covenant oath, sworn to our own hurt, and nailed it to the tree, taking it "out of the way." That is wonderful King James language for: He threw it to the wind!

In His ascension, on His way to be glorified, the principalities and powers tried to grab onto Him to keep Him from His throne and to keep us under bondage to a self-inflicted covenantal oath. He literally shook them off. He took care of the ordinances that were against us and He took care of the principalities and powers that hate us. Hallelujah!

GOD'S ULTIMATE CURE

Neither Adam's nor Israel's failure deflected God from securing His rest in His creation. He assumed initiative where humanity failed. In the New Covenant, God secured His own interests. As with Abraham, He secures His own covenant with Himself. The soil of the covenant is the soul of humanity. Cutting and ratifying the covenant took place at Calvary. In the New Covenant God promises to breathe the very spirit of His life and law into and through the whole inward being of humanity.

The great New Covenant passage of Scripture is Jeremiah 31:27-34. It is quoted apostolically in Hebrews 8:8-12 and 10:16-17. In the passage, God's initiative and determination is seen in the "I wills" of God.

> *Behold, the days come, saith the Lord, that **I will** sow the house of Israel and the house of Judah with the seed of man, and with the seed of beast. And it shall come to pass, that like as I have watched over them, to pluck up, and to break down, and to throw down, and to destroy, and to afflict; so **I will** watch over them, to build, and to plant, saith the Lord. In those days they shall say no more, The fathers have eaten a sour grape, and the children's teeth are set on edge. But every one shall die for his own iniquity; every man that eateth the sour grape, his teeth shall be set on edge. Behold, the days come, saith the Lord, that **I will** make a new covenant with the house of Israel, and with the house of Judah: Not according to the covenant that I made with their fathers in the day that I took them by the hand to lead them out of the land of Egypt; which My covenant they broke, although I was an husband unto them, saith the Lord. But this shall be the covenant that **I will** make with the house of Israel. After those days, saith the Lord, **I will** put My law in their inward parts, and write it in their hearts; and **will** be their God, and they shall be My people. And they shall*

*teach no more every man his neighbor, and every man his
brother, saying, Know the Lord: for they shall all know
Me, from the least of them unto the greatest of them, saith
the Lord: For **I will** forgive their iniquity, and **I will**
remember their sin no more (Jeremiah 31:27-34).*

The "you will" or "you must" expectation of the Old Covenant is
simply not present in these passages. God in Christ by the Holy Spirit has
secured for Himself a beachhead in the soul of humanity. From the beachhead stronghold of the indwelt Christ, a life of obedience begins to flow.
The issue is not an instantaneous transformation. It is one of life flow.

ATTRIBUTES OF THE NEW COVENANT

If through the new birth we are regenerated and become participa-
tors in the New Covenant, we should manifest qualities of life that the
New Covenant itself says we should. If we do not, I question the nature of
the alleged conversion. The passage at hand outlines what a partner in the
New Covenant should both experience and manifest.

KNOWLEDGE (JER. 31:34)

As simple as this may sound, one of the distinguishing characteristics of the New Covenant is the knowledge of God: from the least to the
greatest. It means that in the era of the New Covenant there will no longer
be a need to look to, or for, an external code to ascertain the knowledge
of God. A direct immediate consciousness and familiarity with God is
something God Himself will grant through inward perception. It also
means a mediating class of interpreters (priests) will no longer be needed.
The New Covenant will be characterized by individual personal relationship with God. "God knowledge" will be the common birthright of every
individual.

After 500 years of Protestant teaching we can unconsciously
embrace an attitude of "Well, what's the big deal about that—knowing
God?" If we remember the cultural context of this statement we will
appreciate its cosmic significance. In an era when only a few special
individuals—male prophets or priests—could claim any sort of direct,
immediate contact with Yahweh, this New Covenant promise was
nothing less than radical.

It is important to accurately ascertain what is meant when the
Scriptures use the English term *knowledge*. For most of us reading this

page who come from a Western mindset, knowledge is an intellectual function: the correct apprehension of facts, truth or falsehood, about a person or thing. That is not biblical.

In Hebraic thought, knowledge is neither mental contemplation nor emotional ecstasy. It is experience from relationship, fellowship, and concern. In the New Testament period one of the words used for knowledge is *epígnosis*. It is more than mere intellectual understanding. It is clear and precise knowledge because it expresses a more thorough participation in the object of knowledge on the part of the knowing subject.[6]

> *And this is life eternal that they might know Thee the only true God, and Jesus Christ, whom Thou hast sent* (John 17:3).

In John 17:3 the apostle links eternal life with the knowledge of God. John follows Hebraic thought. Knowledge in John is experiential, intimate, personal, mutual participatory relationship—ascertaining truth concerning God by observation, care, and recognition with immediate understanding. This is the kind of knowledge the New Covenant promises!

Knowledge of God is our response to His character as manifested through relationship and obedience. Knowing God is not orthodox creed or belief, but firsthand knowledge of Him through experience, as framed by the Word of God. It is not merely seeing or understanding principles, ideas, and concepts, but coming to fullness by knowing the Person of Christ through the Person of the Holy Spirit. ***Interaction with God in His Personhood that results in obedience is "knowledge."***

REST (JER. 31:34)

The curse of performance-based religion is the lack of rest. It is a scandal that those who proclaim to have knowledge of God are often stricken with more anxiety, fear, and inner turmoil than those who do not even know Christ! I have met scores of tormented individuals in the Lord's Church—not tormented by the devil, but tormented by ***themselves*** and philosophies of religion that are guaranteed to produce introspective anxiety.

A spirit of rest results from the New Covenant promise to deal with sin once and for all. God promises to deal with it and remember it no more. It is sometimes difficult for a modern Christian to understand the uncertainty with which the Old Covenant saints lived in the Mosaic order. All their hope was focused on the Day of Atonement. If God did not accept their priest and scapegoat on that day, they were still guilty in their sin and under the wrath of God. A faithful Israelite looked to the Day of Atonement like a giant Alka Seltzer—relief for sin was only assured on that day. The promise of the sin issue being dealt with "once and for all" would have been incredibly comforting, assuring, and restful to the first readers of Jeremiah's prophecy. They would have welcomed a day where the covenant sons and daughters could rest in His love as He rested in it over them (see Zeph. 3:16).

Often individuals who obsess about seeking the will of God are the most anxiety prone. How does something that is supposed to be delightful— our relationship, interchange, and communion with our Heavenly Father—deteriorate into an anxiety-laced process of inner torture? How has communion of the Holy Spirit turned into divine lotto, hoping by chance to hit the right number so God can dispense His revealed will to the lucky few? It occurs at the hands of the well-meaning who inject performance-based religion into the blood stream of the Church.

LOVE (JER. 31:27)

The New Covenant is characterized by the covenantal love of Yahweh. His very name—Yahweh—means the God who keeps covenant love, loving-kindness, a love that "stoops down." He is the one who becomes to humanity what they need in every moment.

There is hardly a subject that is more intellectually insipid from overuse than the love of God. Through familiarity and mishandling by generations of tepid preaching, the love of God has been stripped of its cosmic virility and been turned into a sentimental pile of "feel-good," pop psychology goo. Oprah talks about God's love. Dr. Phil talks about God's love. Rosie talks about God's love. The therapists of our culture—the new priesthood for the post-modern mind—have hijacked it. The safe harbor of God's love has been severed from its biblical mooring in His holiness.

The biblical love of God is rooted in God's holiness and manifested in Christ's sacrifice. The new cultural love of God is rooted in "God's affections." God's "unconditional love" is very conditional. Indeed, He loved us while we were sinners. But apart from Calvary (God's eternal "condition"—the Lamb slain from before the foundations of the world) there is no love of God, just the certainty of His holy wrath. Stripping God's love of its Calvary constituency is to betray the Gospel.

> Beware of the pleasant view of the Fatherhood of God—God is so kind and loving that of course He will forgive us. That sentiment has no place whatever in the New Testament. The only ground on which God can forgive us is the tremendous tragedy of the Cross of Christ; to put forgiveness on any other ground is unconscious blasphemy...Never accept a view of the Fatherhood of God if it blots out the Atonement.[7]

Experiencing the *Calvary love* of God—that He loves me, likes me, values me, esteems me in my personhood *in Christ* before the foundations of the world—is key to freedom from performance-based religion. It is the cornerstone revelation necessary to overcome a legal spirit. The love of God is not a theological abstraction that keeps me out of hell. It is the substance of spiritual reality by which I know God and share His life. I am partner with Christ in the love of God. The quality of love that the Messiah, the second Person of the Godhead, the Son of God Himself shares with the Father is *mine*...freely given (see John 17:23; 20:17). Hallelujah!

CHARACTER DEVELOPMENT (JER. 31:28)

The New Covenant is not just a static positioning of favor before God, acquittal of the guilt of sin. It also has to do with our character and strength in the Lord. The ashes of our former life should experience the rebuilding and beautification of the Lord. The New Covenant takes broken people and puts them back together again. It is not about finding broken people and piling principles on them telling them how much they have to change to make God happy. When the life of the New Covenant comes into the heart of a human being, by its nature and essence it begins to beautify. It cannot help but do so as it *is* the life of God. The question for the believer is whether or not to yield to the beautification process.

If I planted grass seed in my yard and walked over it every day after the moment of planting, the problem is not with the seed or the process, but what I am doing to hinder the process. There is no lack of life or power in the seed. If treated right, it will produce. I do not produce the growth. I cooperate with the potential that is in the seed.

So it is with the character-transforming power of the New Covenant. I am not responsible to produce character transformation out of my Adamic resources. I am responsible to cooperate with the Spirit of God's Son in me. The way I do that is to yield to His impressions of life, the quiet inner voice, the nearly imperceptible urges of "don't do that."

It is so easy to ride roughshod over the voice of the Holy Spirit. While His voice is not delicate and fragile, it is still. My reason readily overpowers His inner urgings. The voice of common sense and reason pushes the voice of the Spirit into the back room of my soul where he politely sits and minds His business until He is invited out again by the homeowner. The process of character transformation is not unlike having a radio dial reset.

Before conversion I am utterly dialed into Adam at 50,000 watts at 650 MHz. But as I leave the sphere of Adam and begin to come into the sphere of the Spirit, my inner radio begins to pick up a new but faint signal: the spirit of the Son of God at 100,000 watts, 1410 on the dial. As I adjust my receiver (also known as trial, testing, and transition) to more clearly tune to 1410, the Adamic signal no longer can compare or register. It is simply overwhelmed by the signal strength of the new station and the position of my radio dial—transformation.

PURITY (JER. 31:33-34)

I find it curious to see the secular and spiritist pagan culture of our times co-opt certain elements of Christian vocabulary and adapt them to suit their purposes. Every pagan and cult and new age group believes that "God is love." What distinguishes Christianity is that not only is God love, but He is also holy. The pagans want His love, but not His holiness. One of the characteristics of the genuine experience of the New Covenant life is holiness or purity.

If it is really God's life and Spirit that is in us, His Spirit is holy and we will manifest what has been put in us. To proclaim to be Spirit-filled but to have no manifestation of the purity of God's character in one's life is simply an impossible spiritual incongruity. Again, I am not endorsing instantaneous spiritual perfections. I am talking baby perfections. A newborn is perfect as a newborn, not perfect as an adult.

New Covenant purity is the inherent quality of His Spirit that is given to us when we are regenerated at the new birth. It is received as a gift and responded to, not pumped up or earned. It also removes the stain and condemnation associated with a guilty conscience. We do not have just the judicial putting away of sin, a divine refusal to look at it or reckon it. We have a conscience purged of sin consciousness and the removal of sin's pollution. This results in a clear vision of God. Heart purity is the condition for the knowledge of God[8] as maintained fellowship is the condition for immediate illumination.

PERSONAL POSSESSION/IDENTITY AND BELONGING (JER. 31:33)

The issue of identity has recurred throughout this writing and I have dealt with it in detail in earlier portions of this book. By way of reiteration at this point, the New Covenant promises the believer psychological wholeness, *shalom*[9] well-being, by the experiential reality of knowing that he or she belongs to God. God's desire is relationship and "possession": "They shall be My people." Being God's possession is the privilege of the covenant relationship, and from it, the believer should discover not only the psychology of rest and identity, but also the place of rest: I am in Him and He is in me; I am His and He is mine. I am at rest in His bosom, His heart. We share a name and identity.

A HUSBAND TO ISRAEL (JER. 31:32)

The image of God relating to His people as a husband does his wife recurs through both Testaments. The image is so rich with application that it is worthy of a complete book itself. I will discuss the one metaphor Paul uses in Romans 7 describing the believer's relationship to the law, law living, or principled living.[10]

Romans 7 says that trying to live by principle and law and being "wed' to Christ at the same time is equivalent to having two husbands! Spiritual adultery! You cannot be married to both. Wow! Strong language directed by the apostle to the legalist and performance-based religionist. Christ's death has broken the bond the law had to the Adamic nature in me. In the New Covenant, I am free from my first harsh husband and I am free to remarry: Christ. The key to this passage is to understand why the bond has been broken and a new husband, Christ, has been taken: *to bring forth fruit!*

Oswald Chambers speaks of the need to rescue obedience from the mire of servant and master thinking to Father-Son thinking.[11] Successful Kingdom living, obedience, will not result from scrupulous and legal living but through the manifested realization of our new union with Christ and relationship to the Father. The glorious New Covenant, the promise made long ago to Jeremiah, is that Yahweh will establish a new relationship with His people: not a covenant made upon rules, regulations, and adherence to them, but a covenant akin to marriage. Yahweh Himself will take His bride by the hand and lead her into experiential knowledge with Him.

How did Christ break the bond of the law, the legal claims of God's own law on His creation? Through His work on the cross he has *abolished the law*.[12]

In our culture, *abolish* connotes "gone, out of existence." That is not what it means in the Scriptures. The English word abolished is translated from the Greek word *katargéo* (kat-arg-eh'-o). Here are some of its many-faceted meanings:[13]

- to render idle, unemployed, inactivate, inoperative

- to cause a person or thing to have no further efficiency

- to deprive of force, influence, power

- to cause to cease, put an end to, do away with, annul, abolish

- to cease, to pass away, be done away

- to be severed from, separated from, discharged from

- loosed from any one

- to terminate all intercourse with one

It is possible for something to exist but to have no effect. God's moral law has not disappeared. The standard of God's holiness has not disappeared in the New Covenant. However, through Christ's work and the indwelling Spirit, the law has been rendered inoperative, not non-existent. This helps us understand Paul's perplexing statement about falling from grace (see Gal. 5:4).

For many years I was somewhat troubled by this verse because I took it to mean to lose one's salvation. However, if you look at the context of the verse, and remember to whom he was writing,[14] you can see that it is not talking about salvation. It is comparing those who are trying to justify themselves through works versus those who are trusting Christ. What Paul is saying is that if we do not trust in Christ through faith and grace, the "default position" we will "fall to" is legal living: performance-based religion, trying to appease God by our works. We will have, in effect, fallen from grace to the law.

There are three realms: sin, law, and grace. Living legally is better than sinning out rightly, but living under grace is better than living legally. To fall from grace means I have stepped out of the highest realm and dropped to the next one down. It is like stepping out of an airplane. As long as I am in the airplane, the law of aviation renders the law of gravity ineffectual. The law of gravity has been "abolished." However, if I decide to step out of the plane, the law that was abolished—rendered ineffective by a higher law—suddenly takes hold of me and I have a high-speed appointment with terra firma. This is exactly Paul's logic in Romans chapters 7 and 8. The law has not vanished. A greater law has rendered it ineffective. Its bond on me has been broken. Now, I can choose to resurrect that bond and live like a spiritual bigamist if I want to, but it is not because I have no power to do otherwise. The law of the Spirit of life in Christ Jesus has set me free from the law of sin and death.

WHAT HAS CHANGED?

The problem with the Old Covenant was not the Old Covenant. It was with humanity. The heart of man was not right with God. The New Covenant remedies humanity's *condition*; it *does not alter* or change God's requirement for holiness. In the New Covenant God simply obtains His own ends without dependency on humanity for a contributing portion. The purpose of the New Covenant is so that God's law would be written *in us*. It is not the absence of holiness—it is the presence of His law written in our hearts, released by the Spirit of the Son in us. Holiness is not the absence of sin. It is the presence of the Lord. Wherever He is, is holy. His presence in us sanctifies us. His life in us enables us. Since love thinks no ill toward its neighbor, the love of God and the love of others is the summation of the law (see Gal. 5:14).

The New Covenant is not a change in God's requirement, eternal purpose, or expected end. It *is* a change in and of:

- **Location:** external restraint to internal motivation

- **Material:** from stone to flesh

- **Result:** external conformity to rules to character transformation according to the nature of God.

- **Discipline:** not freedom from discipline, but empowerment to discipline

- **Awareness:** not the absence of God's laws, but the presence of God's laws in our heart

- **Consciousness:** from sin consciousness to Christ consciousness.

- **Source:** obedience from the Adamic nature to obedience from the gift of the indwelling Spirit, the new nature.

RESPONDING TO THE NEW COVENANT

The outcome of the New Covenant is that humanity will understand that God and His ways are good and respond to Him. Humanity's required response is the response of faith, not performance and striving. Faith is the work of God (see Heb. 11:1; John 6:29). Wherever God finds faith, He can do anything. The warfare of our faith, the work of our faith, is the reckoning into and appropriation of the realities of the Christ life within us.

It is no accident that the New Covenant chapter is followed by the account of Jeremiah purchasing a burned-out field in a land that was overrun by an invading army (see Jer. 11–12). After the presentation of Yahweh's glorious promises and "I wills" of the New Covenant, God required Jeremiah to act on something that his senses told him was ridiculous! Now, we are talking real money here. This was not an abstract lesson in theology for Jeremiah. We are talking hard-earned shekels down the tube if what he is hearing from God turns out to be last night's pizza.

Trust validates faith. The nature of faith is like an acrobat pushing a wheelbarrow across Niagara Falls on a tight rope. "Do you believe, I, the Great Zambizi, can do this?" shouts the acrobat. The crowd enthusiastically roars its affirmation. Zambizi then asks for a volunteer from the crowd to get in the wheelbarrow and make the trip with him. Silence sweeps over the crowd like a London fog. Believing Zambizi can do it is a strongly held conviction. Getting in the wheelbarrow is participatory trust—in biblical terms: faith.

We claim to have faith or belief. What we really have is strongly held convictions concerning thoughts about God. God has to destroy our determined confidence in our own convictions.[15] If we obey what God says according to our sincere belief, God will break us from those traditions that misrepresent Him.[16] The destruction process can send a believer into a tailspin if he or she does not understand what is going on. The Lord is trying to get us out of our intellect and into His wheelbarrow. Faith only occurs when you engage Him in His Personhood in the realm of trust when your life is on the line.

For us, faith is a noun, a thing—faith. In John's Gospel, it is never a noun. It is a verb. It is always an action word *pisteúon eis*: to believe into, trusting into. Biblical faith always has an object and has action (obedience) in or toward the object. Saving faith literally believes *into* Jesus Christ.[17] Jesus said that if we love Him, we would obey Him (see John 14:21). Love is manifested in sacrificial acts of service, not feeling or personality.

New Covenant faith is not the mindless, cavalier repetition of biblical verbiage, mental agreement with biblical propositions; nor is it a philosophy of passivity and disengagement—eternally "waiting on God." It is a covenant of action: hear from God and act. That is the New Covenant. A philosophy of waiting on God that is rooted in insecurity and a lack of sonship assurance is not the ethos of the New Covenant. Faith expresses doubt in His presence (not among man—as we learn in Jeremiah and Habakkuk), and obeys Him anyway. If we really believe, we act.

Reckoning and appropriating faith presents to the Lord all that we experience in life that seems contrary to His decrees. In His presence we set up a watch to see what He will answer. Faith is the act of refusing to view God through circumstances, but allows God to enable us to see our circumstances through Him. A burned-out field looks like a bad investment. But, ah, Lord God! You have made the heavens and earth! Is there anything to hard for You? The New Covenant is the answer to Jeremiah's question. There is nothing too hard for Him—not even the human heart.

CONCLUSION

The New Covenant was meant to be a security and guarantee that the things promised would come about. God accomplishes His own purposes by sharing His eternal life with us in the power of covenant. In entering into covenant with us through Christ's sacrifice, God's objective is to draw us to Himself, to render us entirely dependent upon Him, and to participate with Him in the quality of eternal life. The New Covenant inheritance is pardon for sin, having God as our God, divine teaching, and the joint participation in God's very life: eternal life in the power of a divine covenantal oath.

The proof that we are participating in the New Covenant promise is both desire and ability to walk in obedience to God. If we have no passion for God and His ways, we are not saved. A baby is not perfect, but it does have passion for its mother's breast. The converted soul has forever been aligned to God. This does not mean we arrive at sinless perfection at conversion. Nor does it mean we will never experience travails or struggles of the soul, good days and bad days, seasons of encouragement, seasons of discouragement. But it does mean that through the New Covenant's indwelling Spirit, the compass of a human's heart has been forever adjusted toward God. God's Person is the lodestar of the converted soul.

End Notes

1. My personal conviction is that those issues are at the bottom of the Lord's priority list. These are cultural offenses, not biblical offenses. The reaction to alcohol is utterly a phenomenon of American Fundamentalism. It is a non-issue in Christian communities in other cultures around the world. It certainly was a non-issue in Jesus' time. Drunkenness was, and is, a sin. Drinking alcohol is not. Likewise for tobacco. There is not a single verse in the Scripture that deals explicitly with the matter. The verse usually used to address the subject is inferential concerning the body as the temple of the Holy Spirit. I just don't understand the folks who hammer smokers with that verse, thinking nothing of the pollutants and preservatives they defile the temple with every day on their way to obesity and early death. It is the height of hypocrisy for a Christian whose diet is out of control and filling him- or herself with all manner of chemicals, or a nasty tongue-wagging gossiper—a destroyer of the Body of Christ—to lecture a smoker on "defiling the temple of God." Now, exercising one's "liberty" in these areas may be the stupidest thing in the world to do, not helping one's testimony in our culture and playing dangerously close to the line of sin, but until the line is crossed, you are just being stupid, not sinning. Part of the glorious liberty of the sons of God is the freedom to be as stupid as you want to be. If you want to see what sins are on the Lord's radar, compare the seven abominations in

Proverbs 6 to the "American version" of the same: homo-sexuality, abortion, alcohol, tobacco, rock music, Power Rangers, and Cabbage Patch dolls.

2. This is the meaning of the biblical metaphor of head or headship. Of the seven verses in the Scripture that refer to Christ as Head, none of them have anything to do explicitly with authority. They are all relational/body metaphors emphasizing His connectedness and responsi-bility for the body. He is the source and fountainhead of life. Reading "authority," or "authority over," into these passages is cultural bias (see 1 Cor. 11:3; Eph. 1:22; 4:15; 5:23; Col. 1:18; 2:10, 19).

3. A city boy in a country outhouse for the first time—that's a scary scenario.

4. All the New Covenant Scriptures (see Jer. 31:27-34; 32:38-40; Ezek. 36:25-28) mention nothing about going to heaven when we die. Paul is surprisingly silent on the subject of "going to heaven when we die," though he speaks of the realm of heavenlies often. The New Covenant experience is not about hanging on for our final ride into eternity. It is about experiencing the qual-ity of God's eternal life in the present.

5. Oswald Chambers, *My Utmost for His Highest* (Westwood: Barbour and Co., Inc., 1963), p. 5.

6. Spiros Zodhiates, *The Hebrew-Greek Key Study Bible* (Chattanooga: AMG Publishers, 1988).

7. Chambers, *My Utmost*, p. 325.

8. "Blessed are the pure in heart, for they shall see [know, experience] God" (Matt. 5:8).

9. Wellness in all dimensions of existence.

10. It is critical for New Testament doctrine to note that Paul is not making any attempt in this passage to address the sensitive area of divorce and remarriage. It is simply not his topic at hand. In Romans 7, Paul is using a literary device called "limited analogy": drawing application from one topic to another. It is a mistake theologically

and exegetically to make broad application from limited analogy. Great care must be taken.

11. Chambers, *My Utmost*, p. 201.

12. "For He is our peace, who hath made both one, and hath broken down the middle wall of partition *between us*; having abolished in His flesh the enmity, *even* the law of commandments *contained* in ordinances; for to make in Himself of twain one new man, *so* making peace" (Eph. 2:14-15). "And not as Moses, which put a veil over his face, that the children of Israel could not steadfastly look to the end of that which is abolished" (2 Cor. 3:13).

13. Taken from *Thayer's Greek-English Lexicon of the New Testament, Vine's Complete Expository Dictionary of Old and New Testament Words and The Complete Word Study New Testament*.

14. Believers who were being pressured to forsake Christianity and embrace Judaism, or at least a Judaizing form of Christianity.

15. Chambers, *My Utmost*, p. 29.

16. Chambers, *My Utmost*, p. 117.

17. See John chapter 3 in Greek.

Galatians: The Battle for the Mystery, Part One

Discussing legalism without mentioning Galatians is like trying to understand art without Rembrandt. Galatians is *the* Pauline masterpiece on the subject. We have briefly looked at some Galatian themes elsewhere in this book. It is time to examine them in more detail. A verse-by-verse examination would be a worthy safari, but it is a luxury that space and scope do not afford. Although we cannot scour the complete Galatian savannah, I still would like to bring home the big one: the spirit of performance-based, legalistic religion. Jesus already bagged it at Calvary. Paul skinned it in Galatia. It is up to us to make their efforts our trophy. A few word studies and some cultural insights will help us tack that baby up in the den of His victory in our soul.

PAUL'S PASSION

The Book of Galatians has attracted Protestant attention for centuries.[1] It has been called the Magna Carta of the faith and the epistle of Christian liberty. My premise is that Paul's theme is not primarily a doctrinal defense of justification by faith. Justification by faith is a subordinate element of a far greater theme: the battle for the revelation of the mystery.

Although word frequency is not an ultimate determination of theological significance, it does indicate a degree of emphasis. The words *justify, justified*, or *justification* appear only a total of 8 times in 6 verses in Galatians. The Person of Jesus Christ is referred to 60 times—Christ: 39, Jesus: 16, Son: 4. If references to the Spirit are included (see Rom. 8:9;

1 Pet. 1:11), the total jumps to 76—nine times more references to Christ and the Spirit than the doctrine of justification! Approximately 17 percent of the letter's content (one chapter out of six) deals directly with justification, while 83 percent addresses other issues! Like the Whos in Whoville,[2] the great themes of Galatia are yelling "We are here, we are here!"—trying to get the attention of the 3,000-pound elephant of Protestant over-emphasis of justification.

God's eternal purpose has always been that the universe would be a vehicle for divine expression—specifically Christ's expression. Forgiveness of sin is only the first step (albeit a *vital one*) that God the Father needed in order to realize His dream for Christ the Son: winning the nations to obedience and filling the universe with the manifest display of Christ (see Ps. 2; Rom. 16:25; Col. 1:16; 3:11; Eph. 4:10).

Paul refers to the Christ-centered Gospel message as the mystery.[3] The *fact* of the inclusion of the Gentiles into God's plan was no mystery. Anyone could read Isaiah and Hosea and understand God's great determination. The mystery, and its *offense*, is *how* God accomplished His determination and the fact that it must be revealed.

By the gift of the indwelling Spirit, God recreated for Himself a new humanity, a new race in the earth (not in heaven), free of all class and ethnic distinctions: the One New Man (see Eph. 2:15). It is constituted and conformed according to Christ, the Eternal Pattern Man. It is the universal Church, the fullness of Him who fills all in all.

Paul states explicitly that the One New Man mystery is *the* cause for which he dedicated his life and became a prisoner of the Lord Jesus. His burden was the preaching of the Gospel *according to the revelation of the mystery*, that he might make all men see what is the fellowship of the mystery (see Eph. 3:9; 4:1).

Paul's response to a local assembly that was threatened by performance-based religion was to unveil the fellowship of the mystery. The preeminence of Christ and the reality of the Holy Spirit is the apostolic antidote for legalism.

THE ARENA OF BATTLE

Galatians is Paul's first written record of his introduction to the spiritual animosity and resistance to the essence of the revelation of the mystery from *within the community of believers*.[4]

Personal rejection from within the community of faith was nothing new to Paul. His relationship with the Corinthian church is one example. He experienced antagonism to his *message* from the Jews and pagans (Rome). However, in Galatians, he finds his *message* under attack from *within* the community of faith.

Animosity directed toward Christ, God incarnate by inherent Deity in a unique and sinless way, continues against those who would dare preach that God's incarnation continues in the Church through the indwelling Holy Spirit. The devil will tolerate a lot of Christian performance: rules, regulations, meetings, works, and external rituals. He will not tolerate people living in the realized benefits of the fellowship of the mystery—expressing the Kingdom of God *in this life, not just in the next*. The Church in heaven is not a present threat to the devil. The Church on earth is supposed to be.

Galatians is a prophetic signpost of the emotion, tactics, and strategy the antichrist will use to neutralize the Church in the last days. The biggest danger to the Gospel in this generation is not the media, fundamentalist Islam, nor humanism in the schools. The enemy to fear is in the Church's bosom: a Gospel that sounds so right, speaks of justification by faith, exhorts to sanctification, uses all the right terms, appeals to orthodoxy, but which, at its core, is opposed to God's earthly agenda for humanity. The enemy is in the house.

THE ENEMY'S TACTICS

If usurpation of Christ was the devil's plan, what was his method? Three words from Galatians 1:6-7 can give us some insight.

"Removed" (Gr. *metatíthesthe*)—the King James Version's rendering is unfortunately weak. The basic meaning is transporting from one place to another—a transfer. However, when used as in Galatians 1:6, it means turning renegade, to desert, to revolt, a political defection, or becoming a turncoat.[5] Note what Paul is saying. Jesus Christ is the object of this revolt. They have turned renegade from Him. Here are believers, a church founded by the apostle himself, who are actually in rebellion and betrayal against their Savior. They could not recognize what they were doing. The problem did not disappear in the first century. It persists in the Church today. The new Pharisee is devoted to the things of God, but alienated from His Person (see John 5:39-42).

"Trouble" (Gr. *tarrássontes*)—The basic meaning of this word is to cause a commotion or agitation—but this is not merely mental agitation. In other words, Paul's reference was not a mental troubling of doctrine. He continues to follow the metaphorical use of the word for turning renegade in verse 6. In this context, to trouble means to cause commotion associated with a revolt or rebellion, to raise seditions, or to shake allegiance. Again, the issue is not one of adherence to thought, but allegiance to a Person—the Galatians were wavering in their allegiance to both Christ and Paul.

"Pervert" (Gr. *metastréphai*)—This means to reverse, change to the opposite, a reversal. It includes the meanings of distortion, or wrenching, but it is actually stronger than those two words. What was happening in Galatia was not merely a distortion, it was an *extreme* distortion—a polar opposite.

These strong words involve personality, will, and emotion. They indicate that Paul was aware that there was a rebellion going on in the churches of Galatia, not merely tolerance of a novel, variant teaching. The false teaching was the intellectual Trojan horse used for a direct, rebellious assault against the Person of Christ and the implications of the temporal realities of His resurrection, ascension, and outpoured Spirit. Paul's reason for alarm is that this rebellion was from within the house of faith.

The typical evangelical approach to Galatians is indicative that the problem is still in the house. Evangelical orthodoxy has been reduced to correct intellectual adherence to doctrinal suppositions, rather than a living and experiential reality of the Person of Christ as administered by the Holy Spirit in our lives and congregations. Though our creeds may be orthodox, Christ is absent from our meetings and our lives. He has been usurped with something very subtle and difficult to discern, but as old as the garden: Spirit-less religion in the name of Christ.

PAUL'S COUNTERPUNCH (GAL. 3)

After presenting his claims to apostleship and authority to speak on the matter in Galatians chapters 1 and 2, Paul launches his methodological offensive in Galatians 3. Earlier we saw that Paul opens with quite an insulting salvo.[6] It is of the utmost importance to note what he appeals to, and what he *does not* appeal to, as he seeks to counter performance-based religion. He did not argue proof texts (at this point). He did not exegete the Torah. He did not *open* with an exposition of the doctrine of justification. He did not rationalize or try to philosophically out-duel the rabbis (at this point). He *first* appeals to the *experiential reality of the Spirit in their midst.*

As I have outlined in earlier chapters, there are many things that cults and false religions can imitate and emulate. However, there is one thing, and only one thing, that the genuine covenant sons and daughters of God should have claim to: the reality of the Spirit in our midst. Only the genuine children of God have His Spirit. Intellectualized adherents of our faith go apoplectic with the mere mention of objective, observable, spiritual reality—dismissing it as mania, fanaticism, delusion, or worse. It didn't seem to bother Paul, and the fact that its bothers us is an indication of how far we have drifted from the apostolic faith.[7]

In verse 5, Paul uses a delightful Greek word to describe how abundantly God has bestowed the Spirit on the Galatians. King James translates it as "ministereth." It is the Greek word *epichoregéo*, a present participle. It comes from a root meaning of "supply" taken from the ancient Greek dramas. In the Greek dramas there was a feature called the chorus. It was the responsibility of the patron or producer of the drama to fully bear the cost of outfitting the members of the chorus: costumes, masks, catering...everything—he bore the burden. *Epi* is a Greek intensifier.

Like the Greek dramas, God has intensely, abundantly, and continually (present participle) outfitted the believers (the Church) with the Spirit as the antidote for performance-based religion! He has personally borne the cost in the death of the Son and lavished the Church in continuing abundance. It is significant that even as the Galatians were defecting from Him, God was still manifesting the Spirit in their midst. This is a bit difficult for performance-based religionists to fathom because they believe power manifestations are the reward for good behavior or other perfections.

Paul's sentiment is this: In the light of all this Spirit abundance, why would *anybody* want to be so *stupid* as to choose performance-based religion? In modern vernacular, "Whatever, ya major losers! Why on earth are you trying to go back to performance-based religion?" The answer must be "bewitchment" (see Gal. 3:1)!

This reasoning does not impact us in our day because in most evangelical churches the objective manifestations of the Spirit are dismissed as Pentecostal emotionalism. Frenetic emotionalism we can do without, but the Spirit of Pentecost we vitally need. Some systems of theology dispensationally delete spirit manifestations, restricting them to the apostolic age, the height of inferential assumption, without a shred of New Testament exegesis to back it up.[8] The teaching contributes to the vulnerability of the believer to legalism.

If we do not experience the Resource that Paul himself appeals to as an antidote for performance-based religion, what recourse do we have? Remedy everything with more teaching: intellectual philosophizing. Without Spirit consciousness and Spirit manifestation, we will operate in the Kingdom out of our human personalities and temperaments. We will be a collection of nice people being nice to people. This is not the definition of the Lord's pneumatic (spirit-empowered) Church.

ABRAHAM'S SEED

After Paul excoriates the Galatians for their vacillation in the presence of overwhelming Spirit manifestation, he begins a discussion that will take up the rest of chapters 3 and 4. By mentioning the Spirit, he has opened a proverbial can of theological worms.

The Jews knew that an outpouring of the Spirit would characterize Yahweh's last day act in His people (see Joel 2). To claim that the Gentiles had received the promise of the Spirit opens up a sensitive theological problem for Jewish theology: the matter is one of inheritance. The inheritance belonged to the covenant sons and daughters of Abraham. The Jews claimed they were Abraham's heirs. Here's the Jewish question: "What are the Gentiles doing with *our inheritance?* If they want our inheritance, they have to be marked (circumcised) like we are, because the mark makes a person a partaker of the covenant."

So Paul has to do several things:

- Establish the Gentiles as the covenant sons of Abraham.

- By their relationship to Abraham, enfranchise them as inheritors.

- Prove that adherence to the terms of the law does not qualify anyone as an inheritor.

- Demonstrate that the Spirit is both the promised inheritance and proof of who are the genuine children of God.

Paul does this by answering some questions and redefining the entire spiritual universe:

- Who is Abraham's seed? It is not the Jews.

- What are the terms of the covenant? It is not obeying the Mosaic law.

- Who are the sons of God, the sons of the covenant? It is not the Jews.

- Who are the heirs? It is not the Jews.

- What is the promise? It is not heaven.

- What is the identity marker? It is not circumcision.

No wonder they wanted to kill him!

HANGING ON GRAMMAR

Our entire faith hinges on Paul's use of a noun. He says that the promise made to Abraham wasn't made to Abraham. It was made to Christ in Abraham's loins (see Gal. 3:16). The promise was made to the Seed, singular, not seeds plural. If Paul is wrong, if the promise is to the seeds, then the Spirit belongs to the natural children of Abraham and the Gentiles are out of luck. The church is a fraud. You and I are dead in our sins, outside the covenant, and alienated from God. If we have not been covenantally and relationally restored to God, then we have no alternative but to work hard, perform, do our best, and hope that we get our pass into heaven when we die. If it is singular, Seed, as Paul said, then whoever is "in Christ" is a covenant son and inheritor.

It is faith that determines sonship, and sonship determines inheritance. Our faith hinges on a dispute of grammar—the presence or absence of the letter "s." Whoever said the devil is in the details sort of had it right. In this case it is God who is the details!

WHO IS YOUR DADDY?

Readers over 40 may remember a song called "Time of the Season"[9] by the U.K. band, *The Zombies*. The lyrics say: "What's your name (what's your name)? Who's your daddy (who's your daddy)? Is he rich, is he rich like me?" I doubt the band had Galatians in mind, but they stumbled upon a profound order of spiritual truth: identity, fatherhood, and riches (inheritance).

In Galatians, Paul expands on these three themes as his antidote for legalistic religion. Why is it important to know who your daddy is? If you can't prove your identity, your link to your father, you can't claim his inheritance. Your daddy may be rich, but if you don't know who you are, or can't prove it, his riches are not yours.

The Judaizers claimed Abraham as their father naturally and Yahweh as their Father spiritually. Through this claim, anything that accrued to Abraham was theirs by inheritance. In their minds, the proof of their claim as covenant sons and heirs was circumcision. If pressed, the Judaizers could swallow the Gentiles' sharing in the covenant and its blessings—but they had to have the identity marker: circumcision. That was as far as the Judaizers could go in embracing this "New Covenant." In a sense, they were trying to be "reasonable" and accommodate between the Old Order and the New Order by mixing a bit of both. "Yes, we believe Jesus was the Messiah. Yes, we believe we are saved by faith, but if you want to share in Abraham's promise, you must be marked with Abraham's mark."

Paul accurately perceived that, in this case, compromise was not the path of largesse and nobility, but the path of destruction. This was leaven he could not endure. Paul said the proof of claim to God-lineage—having Yahweh as Father—was not Abraham's *person*, but Abraham's *faith*. Jesus shared the same thought in John 8:39 when He said the link to Abraham was *behavior*, not genealogy. These 2,000-year-old, seemingly benign propositions were the equivalent of a meteor smashing the theological landscape. They drew a murderous response in the hearers.

The identity marker of the New Covenant is not circumcision. It is the indwelling Spirit available to all humanity through faith. The promise of the Father, the Spirit of sonship in the heart of the believer, is the sign of participation in the covenant and proof of inheritance.

The key to success in overcoming performance-based legalism is knowing our identity so the resources of the inheritance that Christ has left us in the Holy Spirit can be made effectually ours. Merely believing I am forgiven will not do it. Believing I am fully inherited does. And I appropriate my inheritance by pressing my identity claim, not by working harder.

THE TEMPORARY SLAVE MARKET

As if insulting their heritage and religious customs were not enough, Paul further alienates the Jewish brethren by declaring that law-living did not justify or entitle them as inheritors. He told the Galatians that the law was a temporary arrangement until the appearing of the Seed and faith in Him. In Romans 5:20 Paul says the law entered (Gr. *pareisérchomai*) or came alongside faith as the means of being a participator of the covenant. The law was added (Gr. *prostíthemi*) because of transgressions (to make sin exceedingly sinful) until the Seed should arrive.

Not only does Paul say that law-living was temporary, but it also carried with it a curse for any disobedience (see Gal. 3:10). Christ took the curse for us at Calvary and redeemed us from its power.[10] The meaning of redemption is "to be bought out of the slave market." Christ has redeemed us from two forms of slavery: the slavery of sin and the slavery of performance-based religion. Paul later calls perceptual, performance-based, legal code living as the "yoke of bondage" or "the yoke of slavery" (Gal. 5:1). In John 8, Jesus told the Jews the same: They were slaves. Christ has bought us out of the performance-based slave market.

THE INHERITANCE

For as many of you as have been baptized into Christ have put on Christ (Galatians 3:27).

And if ye be Christ's, then ye are Abraham's seed, and heirs according to the promise (Galatians 3:29).

Many evangelical churches preach a very limited Gospel consisting of two basic elements: forgiveness of sins (through faith in Christ's atonement) and assurance of heaven upon death. I am not deriding or minimizing the importance of either. I am glad I am both forgiven and assured of heaven. However, to present only this limited emphasis is very man-centered. It emphasizes the benefits that accrue *to* and *for* humanity through Christ's work on the cross. The essence of Paul's Gospel is Christ-centered: Christ became a curse for us for a *specific reason*.

In Galatians 3:14, Paul uses an interesting Greek conjunction, *hina*. It is a demonstrative word, meaning "so that, in order that, with the purpose of, resulting in, etc." Christ's becoming a curse for us was not to get us to heaven. The reason Christ became accursed is so the Gentiles could receive the blessing of Abraham! The blessing of Abraham is not heaven when we die; nor is it a chunk of real estate in the Mid East. It is the reality of the Spirit! The blessing of Abraham according to apostolic doctrine is the Spirit of Christ in me!

Abraham was promised seed as numerous as sands of the sea and stars of the sky. He was promised that the whole earth would be blessed through him. How are all the nations going to be blessed in Abraham? By the indwelling Spirit, in the heart of every human, without regard to race or class. *The Spirit's infilling, resulting from Christ's resurrection and ascension (see Acts 13:33), is the fulfillment of the promise made to Abraham.*

Out of every tribe, tongue, kindred, and nation the indwelling Spirit makes covenant sons out of rebels and enemies. God put His Spirit upon and within all flesh, not just the literal seed of Abraham. Because you are Abraham's seed, you are fit for Daddy's house and the inheritance is yours! *You are free from performance-based religion!*

Paul spends the rest of chapter 3 expanding on two metaphors, neither of which will endear him to his Jewish listeners. He likens the law and living under the law by rules, precepts, performance, and code, to being under the regime of a jailer or a nag.

THE JAILER

Paul likens waiting for Christ's appearing under the regime of law-living as being "shut up unto faith." Although the metaphor means waiting until faith arrives, the language has more substance than merely passing time. It means to incarcerate someone. The law is a jailer. What's the purpose of a jail? It restrains somebody's nasty behavior. Paul says that the jail is fine for that purpose. But if something better comes along (and it has) that would result in character and behavior change, the jail would no longer be necessary. In the new birth, through the indwelling Spirit, that is what is *supposed* to have happened to humanity.

How many Christians live with the jailer mentality! For them, Christianity is all about the boundaries, limitations, and restrictions: don't go here, don't go there, don't do this, don't do that, don't eat this, don't eat that, don't get caught, stay out of trouble. Christianity becomes an anxiety-ridden, paranoia-filled, suspicion-laced, perfectionistic, judgmental existence of trying to avoid the jailer's scrutiny.

Paul's presentation to the Galatians is that through the gift of the Spirit—the promise of the Father—the believer has been given a new identity and a character change. He makes it clear: the law is temporary, like a jailer who finds himself unemployed because all the criminals have had a heart change. The Liberator Seed has arrived.

THE "NAG"

In Galatians 3:24 English translations speak of law-living as being under a schoolmaster. Although not a bad rendering, because of our cultural assumptions, we can think along this line: "Hey, preach that "grace stuff" and, the next thing you know, people will be living sloppy agape. They will be sinning all over. God gave the law because the law is the teacher. We should use the law to teach people until they mature in Christ." This seems reasonable, yet is utterly flawed at both a theological and cultural level.

In Roman society, the moral instruction and training of sons in their minority was not the responsibility of parents, particularly fathers. The level of paternal disengagement in child rearing in first-century Roman (and Jewish) culture would shock some of our cultural parenting values. By our standards, fathers would be considered inappropriately disengaged. The responsibility for child training fell to a household slave called the pedagogue (*paidagogós*).

In Galatians 3:23, Paul compares the law to the Roman pedagogue. Our language has embraced the term almost in total. Pedagogy is the practice of teaching. The pedagogue's job was not to be a schoolteacher as we might define it: teaching the child the three R's, facts, intellectual development, etc. Roman society had another institution that served that function: the academy.

The pedagogue was responsible for the *moral* upbringing, not the intellectual development of the son or heir. The pedagogue was to act as a moral conscience, not as an instructor. The way the pedagogue accomplished this was with a switch. The pedagogue was to literally shadow the boy everywhere he went. Every time the boy did something morally wrong, the pedagogue was supposed to whap the boy, and repeat a moral axiom. The father in Roman society had the privilege called *patria potestas*: absolute paternal rule.[11] It is the right to do whatsoever he pleased, including the ability to execute slaves. In this light, the pedagogue was highly motivated to do his job well!

Not only did Calvary deal with our sin, our alienation from God, the devil's claim, our eternal judgment, and more, it also dealt with the pedagogue, the whip-and-teach relationship—the law. We have received the Spirit of adoption (discussed in the next chapter). In Christ we have been put into our majority—we are no longer minors on probation. We are fully accepted, mature sons. Since the pedagogue was for minors, he is *no longer our guide*. The indwelling Spirit of the Son is our guide and He doesn't use a switch! He uses His voice. The law is for (teaches) the transgressors (sinners), as Paul says in First Timothy 1:9. The indwelling Spirit teaches the sons and daughters. Unlike the pedagogue who could only point out deficiency and the son's moral responsibility, the indwelt Spirit of the Life of the Son convicts *and* empowers—something the pedagogue could never do.

CONCLUSION

In chapter 4 of Galatians Paul ratchets up counterpunching both in degree of difficulty and intensity. He closes chapter 3 (verses 26-29) in a flurry of profound and cosmologically altering truths. They are the summary underpinning of our victory against legalistic and performance-based religion, the foundations of the Christian faith:

- You are children of God by faith in Christ (Gal. 3:26).

- All the formerly disenfranchised are in on it (Gal. 3:28).[12]

- In Christ the Seed, you are the seed too (Gal. 3:27,29).

- Since you are the seed, you are the heir (Gal. 3:29).

- Since you are the heir, the promise is yours (Gal. 3:29).

- And the promise is the Holy Spirit (Gal. 3:2,14).

No wonder they wanted to kill him.

CHAPTER EIGHT

End Notes

1. It was pivotal in Luther's and Calvin's Reformation theology.

2. Reference to Dr. Seuss's, *Horton Hears A Who.*

3. Rom. 16:25; 1 Col. 2:7; Eph. 3:3-4,9; 6:19; Col. 1:26-27; 2:2; 4:3; 1 Tim. 3:9.

4. Likely written in A.D. 49.

5. Sources: BAGD, Lightfoot's Commentary, Classical Gr. usage.

6. Discussed in Chapter Three of this work.

7. Gordon Fee has said: "The net result has been that the Pauline perspective of life in the Spirit, as a dynamically experienced reality creating an eschatological people who live for God's glory, has not generally fared well in the overall life of the Church." From God's Empowering Presence by Gordon Fee ©1994 by Hendrickson Publishers, Peabody, MA. Used by Permission. All rights reserved.

8. Gordon Strachan writes: "There is no scriptural authority for dividing up the gifts of the Spirit into that which is extraordinary and that which is ordinary; and, upon the strength of the arbitrary division to say the former was never intended to continue but the latter only." From The Pentecostal Theology of Edward Irving by Gordon

Strachan © 1973 by Hendrickson Publishers, Peabody, MA. Used by Permission. All rights reserved.

D. Martin Lloyd-Jones writes: "Anyone who cuts out portions of Scripture is guilty of very grievous sin"; and "Anyone who is prepared to say that all this [charismatic manifestation] ended with the apostolic age, and that there has never been a miracle since the apostles, is making a most daring statement. Not only is there nothing in Scripture to say that all these miraculous gifts had to end with the apostolic age, the subsequent history of the church, it seems to me, gives the lie to this very contention." From The Sovereign Spirit by D. Martyn Lloyd Jones © 1985 by Harold Shaw Publishers, Wheaton, IL. Used by permission.

D.L. Moody writes: "When He comes He will confirm His Word with signs following"; and "He has left to us the same power He possessed." From Secret Power by D. L. Moody © 1973, Gospel Light/Regal Books, Ventura, CA 93003. Used by Permission.

F.F. Bosworth writes: "Why would the Holy Spirit, Who healed all the sick before His dispensation began, do less after He entered office? Did the Miracle-Worker enter into office to do away with the miracles during His own dispensation?" From Christ the Healer by F. F. Bosworth © 1973 Fleming H. Revell Co. Public Domain.

9. Rod Argent and Chris White, *The Zombies*.

10. The Scriptures use three words for redemption: *agorázo*, to buy in the slave market; *exagorázo*, to buy a slave out of the slave market; *lutróo*, the ransom money used to buy a slave out of the slave market. Christ has done all this for us.

11. Some men in the church think this is what being "head" of the woman or "head of the family" means. This is a gross distortion. The biblical head is servant of all, the one who is called to lay down his life for others, not exercise alleged privileges of an alleged "position of authority." Misguided men who think being head is

about "ruling" their wife and family are actually pagan in their thinking, even with the Bible under their arm.

12. Women, Gentiles, and slaves were the three classes in Jewish society who were disenfranchised, without rights or direct access to God.

Galatians: The Battle for the Mystery, Part Two

"HOT DOG."

Without surrounding context, it is impossible to determine the meaning of these two words. With changes in voice inflection, this simple phrase can mean different things to the hearer. If I emphasize neither word, it is what I eat at the ballpark. If I emphasize both words, it means I am excited about an opportunity or proposition. If I let my voice tail off at the end of each word, and add a tone of disdain, it is a negative comment about showboating behavior. If George Washington had used the phrase, he would have meant his neighbor's overheated spaniel. The meaning of this simple phrase is determined by context and culture. The same difficulties apply to Scriptural interpretation.

"The Bible says it, I believe it, and that settles it" is a bumper-sticker mantra of fundamentalist fidelity for some. I have often thought that the bumper sticker should be sold in a matched set with a companion that reads: "And I can't be bothered to think and study!" I am amazed at the market for advertised ignorance. To even question the legitimacy of this saying might raise suspicious eyebrows that a closet "liberal" may be lurking in the interpretive bushes.

Of course, the same people (usually men) who slap this on the back side of their car, feel no twinge of interpretive conscience to pass on the biblical injunctions to greet one another with a kiss, or to drink a little wine for stomach infirmities, or to hate one's parents to follow Jesus—each a "biblical" instruction. The reason consciences remain calm and the guardians of biblical integrity are not aroused at these admonitions is because it is "obvious" these verses do not apply to us today.[1] Obviousness is in the eye of the beholder. Determining from Scripture what is universal and trans-cultural in application and what is only local and intra-cultural without any contemporary application, is *the* interpretive challenge—the equivalent of theological nuclear war—no survivors, and blood on the floor.

WHAT'D HE SAY?

We must remember that when we read the New Testament, we are reading somebody else's 2,000-year-old mail. We are crashing in on a conversation without the benefit of similar language, background, history, culture, and context. I think it would behoove us to be a bit slow to speak about what we *think* we understand a given passage of Scripture to mean. Simply because I may have a ninth grade American education, and the King James Bible under my arm, does not necessarily mean that I will correctly understand what is in there! Indeed, a five-year-old can understand those things necessary for salvation. However, attempting to faithfully believe and live by the Scriptures will require more than milk, cookies, and an afternoon nap if we are to avoid some very peculiar ideas and behaviors that are allegedly "biblical."

One of the cornerstone principles[2] of conservative, Protestant, biblical interpretation that I continually emphasize in my local church is the ***principle of originality***. Before we attempt to apply the Scriptures to ourselves, we must do the very best we possibly can, using every tool and resource we can, to understand them *first* in terms of what the original author and hearers intended and understood.

Whatever our position might be on a passage of Scripture (particularly a controversial one) one thing is certain: *Any interpretation that would have been impossible or unintelligible to the original hearers **cannot** be the literal meaning of the passage.* There *may be* application beyond the original literalness (particularly where prophetic Scripture occurs). However, we best start with understanding what was *sure* in the minds of the author and hearer *before* we jump to conclusions and applications for ourselves.

Galatians 4 is Paul's final argument against performance-based religion.[3] He parries and thrusts his way through his opponents, dismissing them with a final theological *coup de grace* of metaphors and allegories in which he presumes upon mutual understanding in his hearers.[4] That is not the case for the 21st century, Western, first-time reader.

Nowhere is this principle more apt than in Galatians 4. It is universally regarded as one of Paul's most difficult chapters to understand. It is difficult conceptually and culturally. There are literally hundreds of opinions about it in the commentaries. In it, Paul refers to Hebrew Scripture and practice, Greek culture and language, and Roman law and culture to make his case. These things were the air of their day-to-day existence. What was air to breathe for them is mud to slog through for us. We do not share the same culture, language, societal structure, ethics, and legal system. It makes for a very challenging pot of interpretive biblical goulash.

If we are to appreciate the full force of Paul's closing presentation, we must briefly examine some background cultural information. With the Holy Spirit's invaluable assistance, we can try to understand as much of Paul's passionate argument as possible as he speaks of:

- Two Covenants
- Two Heirs
- Two Sons
- Two Methods of Birth
- Two Emissaries
- Two "Mothers"
- Two Cities

GROWING PAINS

Having dealt with issues of identity, sonship, fatherhood, and inheritance in chapter 3, Paul continues and adds a new dimension, addressing a slightly different but related question: What does it mean to be spiritually mature and how do I get there?

The Judaizers were not categorically challenging the legitimacy of the Galatian's faith. They were presenting a Gospel message that said, "We accept your faith in Messiah as saving, but to 'really please God,' you must do certain things in addition to believing in Jesus as Christ and Lord." Their premise was that the believer who is really a mature son, passionate for God, etc., will demonstrate it by certain actions and deeds. In their case it was conformity to Jewish religious practices, specifically circumcision and Sabbath and feast observance. In our time it can be any dutiful, mechanical, hair-splitting, nit-picking behavior that someone deems authoritative and binding upon believers in order to "walk in righteousness" and "really please God."

The pursuit of spiritual maturity is the number one opening for legalism in the life of the believer. Sometimes, people who have sinned excessively prior to their "conversion" are the most vulnerable to performance-based religion because in their carnality and ignorance, they try to outdo in righteousness what they used to do in wickedness! Personal reformation is not the same thing as the new birth. One is an Adamic process, the other a new creation, a pneumatic (spiritual) process.

The journey of Christian maturity is biblically sanctioned, a legitimate goal. But *how* one makes the trip is the difference between sonship and slavery. One method is the slave galley, chained and stroking to the beat of a performance-based system of rules and regulations. The other is raising the sail of sonship and letting the wind of the Spirit carry us to the destination. Our ship will likely make it into port either way, but one will arrive exhausted and resentful in the slave galley and the other refreshed and encouraged in the sloop of the spirit of sonship.

GROWING UP INTO THE HEAD

Christian maturity is commonly, *and erroneously*, pursued through the acquisition of virtues and the elimination of sins. This may come as a shock to some, but this premise is Buddhist or Gnostic, not Christian. The Buddhist or Gnostic believes that through the denial of self, the purging of evil and negativity, and the acquisition of virtue and enlightenment that he or she will achieve heightened states of spiritual consciousness or Nirvana, shaking off the lower existence of the material realm and achieving union with the spirit realm.

THE NEW STANDARD OF SPIRITUAL MATURITY

Christ, and our participation in and with Him, is the new standard of spirituality since Pentecost. Spiritual maturity is the ***increase of Christ,*** *not the acquisition of virtues*.[5] Adam can dress himself quite primly in the garments of Christian virtue. Christ is the eternal center of the Father's idea of both the goal and method of spiritual maturity. This is the key to overcoming legalism and understanding the entire Gospel. The post-Pentecost order of spiritual maturity is defined by:[6]

1. **The revelation of Christ within** (Col. 1:27)—the fact of the indwelling Christ as my Savior.

2. **The living of Christ within** (Gal. 2:20)—I experience Christ as my life source.

3. **The formation of Christ within** (Gal. 4:19)—my growth and sanctification in Christ.

4. **The abiding (down-sitting) of Christ within** (Eph. 3:17)—maturation, experiencing Christ as my rest.

5. **The consummation of Christ within** (2 Thess. 1:10)—God's glory manifested in and through the believer.

Biblical maturity is defined ***relationally, in Christ,*** not by performance, good or bad. Whenever, wherever, and however Christ is manifested in human flesh, is spiritual maturity. A newborn convert who acts in accordance with the Great Commandment is more mature spiritually than a glow-in-the-dark saint who can check off his "don't do and won't do list,"[7] but who sits at home, relationally disengaged from God's Spirit and others. If my inward, personal character is flawless, but my relationships are out of order, I am yet a spiritual infant.

The Great Commandment is the *fulfillment of all the law and prophets*.[8] Note that it has **nothing to do with the adornment of our personal character**. It is possible, perhaps even desirable (if one had to choose), that someone could be quite deficient in personal character yet excel in this simple Great Commandment.

It does not take a spiritual giant to fulfill this command. Any babe in Christ can fulfill it if he or she embraces death and resurrection life. Spiritual ability flows out of death and resurrection, not character transformation. My character, good or bad, is not the seat of my obedience. The indwelling Spirit of Christ is. Character conformity to the image of Christ is what I will take with me into eternity when I die. Obedience to the Great Commandment is for the here and now. The focus of the Great Commandment is *relational*—God and humanity—and it is *outward*.

THE "MINOR" LEAGUES

In addressing the issue of spiritual maturity or immaturity, Paul uses three images from his contemporary culture. They are pictures of being under authority or under another's influence: a minor child, a slave, and a Roman son or heir. The unifying element of these three is that in Roman society each had no civil rights. They were not mature in a legal sense. Paul is making the case that the performance-based religionist, in spite of all contentions and pretensions to the contrary, is spiritually immature.

A CHILD (GAL. 4:1,3)

This is the Greek term, *népios*. It means one that does not speak, an immature person, intellectually, and morally. A minor child, though potentially an heir, was legally in much the same position as a slave. He could not perform any act or claim any privilege, except through the behest of his legal representative, his father. Unable to exercise his free will, a child must have legal restraint put on him. A child in Rome was, literally, a non-person. He was considered *infantia* until the age of 7. He was under a tutor (*pedagogue*) until puberty, and under a *curater* until he was 25. He only became a son socially and legally when he accepted his sonship in a formal adoption proceeding.

Paul is claiming that the performance-based religionist is intellectually and morally a child. The boundaries and limitations they require for psychological wholeness are not an indication of their maturity, but rather, immaturity. They also promote fear because as soon as I have made a limitation boundary I am aware of it, and aware of the potential for crossing it, which makes me introspective and fearful. A line is there to be avoided.

A SLAVE (GAL. 4:1,7; 5:1)

Slaves in first century Rome constituted a large percentage of the population. Paul likens performance-based religion to slavery. The Greek term is *doûlos*, literally, a bond slave, not merely a house servant, or an indentured servant, but an utter bond slave with no rights. Although not identical to the American slavery experience as we have outlined earlier, slave existence was one of servitude and a lack of liberty. A slave owner, master of a house, could dismiss or execute a bond slave at will.[9] Rome was literally teeming with slaves.

A SON/HEIR (GAL. 4:1,6)

The Greek word is *huiós*. It is a distinctly unique Greek term for a distinctly Roman custom. It means a full-grown or mature son, one that has been endowed with full civil rights through the Roman process of adoption (covered later in this chapter). A *huiós*, though he was the heir, son, and lord in the sense of his father's inheritor, had no more privileges than a slave until he had been "adopted."

ADOPTION DAY

Paul refers to the day of adoption as the "time appointed" (Gal. 4:2). This is a term referring to the formal termination of a son or daughter's minority. In all three ancient cultures of the New Testament—Hebrew, Greek, and Roman—there was a special day and ceremonial ritual for a son (or daughter) to come into his (her) manhood (womanhood) legally and spiritually. For the Jews it is the bar-mitzvah (for males). For the Greeks it was called the *apátouria*, literally (without a father). For the Romans the process was called *adoptio* (from whence we get adoption). Included in the Roman ceremony was a change of garment. The purple robe of a minor was put away for the plain bottomed robe of an adult. The boy brought a ball and a girl brought a doll as a sacrifice to the gods, signifying the putting away of childish things and assumption of adulthood responsibilities.[10]

Adoption was a process through which not only did a son assume his majority, but also a wealthy and childless man could take into his family a slave youth. This youth, by a stroke of good fortune, ceased to be a slave and became a legal son and heir. However, before a slave could be adopted he had to be redeemed. (We shared briefly on this in the last chapter.) The difference between redemption and adoption is that a redeemed slave experienced a change of ownership, but not a change in material condition. Adoption changed his material condition.

When a slave owner wanted to free his slave, he did not simply set him loose as we might think in our culture. A slave's "lot in life" was considered to be the result of the gods' determinations for him.

In order to achieve freedom, the slave owed the gods the cost of his redemption.

> The Greek slave, when he desired to secure his liberty, did not bring his master his earnings and obtain his freedom with his receipt for the money; he went to the temple of the god, and there paid in his money to the priests, who then with this money bought the slave from his master on the part of the god, and he became for the rest of his life a slave of the god— which meant practically freedom, subject to certain periodical religious duties.[11]

At that time, a formal document was drawn up and filed in the temple, which literally read, "for freedom." If at any time his master or his master's heirs claimed him, he had the record of the transaction in the temple. As part of the "freedom" process, the priests in the temple branded the free slave with the mark, the "stigmata," of his new master.[12] Thus, the slave branded as free had not only the temple record, but a physical mark in his body to take with him everywhere, literally, declaring to one and all that he was free.[13] Freedom in first century Rome for a slave was a change in masters: from man to the god(s).

This is why Paul could refer to slavery and freedom in the same verse (see Gal. 5:13). Freedom for a slave in their culture was understood to be a change in masters. So it is in Christian liberty. Liberty is not the absence of governmental restraint. It is a change in governing authority: from submission to sin, the flesh, and the devil, to the Lord in resurrection and His Kingdom. Where the Spirit of the Master is, there is liberty (see 2 Cor. 3:17). We are slaves to a new Master, not free to do whatever it is we please with God's grace. Our redemption price has been paid in the shedding of Christ's blood. The certificate of freedom we carry is the indwelling Spirit who cries *Abba Father* in our heart.

ADOPTION: THE RESULTS

After the slave had been redeemed, he could partake in the Roman adoption process that had three profound consequences— which have implication for believers across all times and cultures:

First, the adopted person lost all rights and relationships with his old family and gained privileges of a fully legitimate son in his new family. He literally assumed a new identity—civilly and legally. He was forever cut off from his former lineage, whatever it may have been. This has been Paul's whole argument throughout. In Christ, the believer has a new identity and a new lineage. He has been re-gened to a new Father. One's natural heritage no longer determines one's lot in life and destiny. The believer is a bona fide new creation. Just as a new civic identity appeared on the Roman law books as a result of adoption, so a new identity has appeared in the eternal records in the Lamb's book of Life, as the result of our adoption into full sonship status in Christ.

Second, the adopted son became a full heir to his new father's possessions. All the father had was his. He had free access to his father's houses and wealth. Even if the father had natural sons after the slave was adopted, they could not disinherit, nor take the adopted son's place. The process of adoption was permanent in all its effect. Once placed as a son, it was an irrevocable condition. The adopted slave was inalienably a joint heir. The believer is forever a joint-heir with Christ (see Rom. 8:17). All of the Father's love and all the riches of His inheritance for us in Christ are available to the new creation son or daughter. This is Paul's argument.

Third, the record of the adopted son's old life was completely wiped out. All debts were canceled as though they never existed. All public records were purged of the former identity and former debts. It is as if the former identity never existed. For the blood-washed saint, judgment day has already occurred. The future judgment that awaited me as a result of the legitimate moral indictments against me has already been poured out on Christ in my place. I have already been condemned, I have died, been buried, and am risen again to newness in Him. My old life's track record has been erased.

For the believer in Christ, the Calvary event is one inclusive act in which we are redeemed and adopted. The believer, by faith and the indwelling Spirit, has been given a new identity. It cannot be improved upon by anything we do or add to our faith. It is a legal transaction that has been paid for with lasting result. The inheritance of our Father, the promise of the Spirit, is legally and actually mine. All my former moral debts are canceled. They literally do not exist.

LEAVING THE ABC'S OF CHILDHOOD

In Galatians 4:3-4, 9, Paul refers to "bondage to the elements of the world" as a beggarly way of life. The elements of the world are the "beginning principles," the ABC's, the things set side-by-side, precept by precept, which Paul calls a form of slavery. Principles have no power to save, no richness, nor endowment. These are strong terms indicating that the Galatians were on the verge of a complete relapse to utter worthlessness. Living by principles is one of the aspects of slavery and bondage from which Christ has set us free. Paul's argument to the Galatians is, "Why would you want to trade beggarly, principled living for the life of a fully inherited son in Him? Why would you want principles instead of the Person?" This was exactly the trade off Israel made at Sinai.

Being a very scrupulous and principled individual is not a sign of spiritual maturity. It is a sign of bondage and immaturity. In Galatians 4:10, Paul says they were, as he was speaking,[14] "minutely and scrupulously observing" outward ordinances and rituals. They were already observing dates, times, and such, and now they wanted to add circumcision. Paul said their non-filial, non-sonship behavior terrified him (see Gal. 4:11)!

TWO EMISSARIES

Paul also speaks of two different "sending forths." The Son Himself was sent forth in the fullness of time (see Gal. 4:4). This word, *exapostéllo*, does not mean sent forth from a place, but rather sent as a pervading influence. It is the language of patronage. The one sent forth represents the qualities of the sender, the place, or the society that sent him. We are all familiar with the sending forth of the Son because of the emphasis on Christmas in our culture. Surely, the Son is the Father's ambassador, representing both the qualities of heaven and the Father's interest.

But Paul also speaks of another sending forth. It again is the language of patronage. The place where the second sending forth has occurred is not in the earth as the Son's sending was, but in the heart of the believer. The Roman adoption ceremony had to be witnessed and announced publicly to be legal and binding. Paul says that the Holy

Spirit, sent forth into the heart of the believer, is the witness and the announcement of adoption! The Spirit himself,[15] with a loud and earnest shout,[16] makes a public announcement that the adoption has occurred! Since the Spirit Himself bears witness, why would anybody doubt or want to go back or embrace performance-based religion? Paul's incredulity is palpable.

ABBA AND IMMA

The result of the sending in the heart is the release of the cry, Abba Father! While many are familiar with the endearing qualities associated with this word, we sometimes lose the significance of it in Paul's context of the adoption ceremony. Slaves were forbidden to use either term, *abba* (daddy/father) or *imma* (mom/mother). They had no legal right to either term, even though they might spend their entire lifetime in a household with the same master. They needed a change in legal status to use the term. This is another benefit that accrues to a slave who has been adopted. He has the right to terms of endearment. For the believer, the self-attesting reality and witness of the Spirit, the fact that we cry *Abba Father* is all the proof we need that we are sons and heirs.

We have not merely been brought into a judicial relationship like a criminal getting parole instead of a death sentence. We have been brought into a familial and filial relationship. God is not merely the judge who has been appeased because Jesus served our sentence. He is our beloved Father and we, His dear children. The judicial aspect of Calvary is surely legitimate, but when emphasized at the expense of the filial, it is a formula for insecurity, bondage, and performance-based religion. If I view myself as a criminal on parole, my status of freedom is only as good as my effort at meeting my terms of parole. If I meet the terms, I maintain my freedom, but cross the line and I am prisoner again. Judicially, I have not been paroled. I have been pardoned and the Judge has taken me on as His beloved son.

THE LAST CHARGE UP MOUNT PERFORMANCE

Beginning at about verse 12 and picking up again at verse 20, Paul changes his tone from one of intensity and incredulity that he had been using, and entreats them with the language of tenderness like a mother who has given her life for her children. He is doing everything he can to appeal to the Galatians. He knows that he is about to lower the boom on them again. He would rather they respond to his tenderness, but so far, it is not going so well. He is now set to go for the jugular in the rest of chapter 4 and the first half of 5. Paul is going to logically and rhetorically take on the Judaizers who were influencing the Galatians and hurl one last, staggering insult at them.[17]

DUELING RABBIS

Beginning in verse 21, Paul puts back on his yarmulke and takes on the Jewish contingent on their own terms: rabbinical interpretation. This is why the passage can be so difficult for us. We do not have Eastern minds and have not been rabbinically trained. The key is to remember that he is speaking rabbi to rabbi. The rabbis handled Scripture in four ways:[18]

- Peshat—the literal meaning

- Remaz—the suggested meaning

- Derush—investigative meaning

- Sod—the allegorical or revelational meaning

Paul is just acting as a good rabbi would. What he is doing, in effect, is using their own methods of handling Scripture to undermine their position. He was giving them a taste of their own medicine by presenting the story of Abraham's family as an allegory for the issue going on in Galatia.

What is his purpose in doing so? Earlier in chapters 3 and 4 he has already told them that they are not part of the covenant, they are not Abraham's seed, Abraham is not their father, they do not have the identity marker, and they are not heirs—proving that he failed the Dale Carnegie course. In a final surge of exhaustion he is now about to say that not only is Abraham not their father, but Sarah is not their mother. He attacked both sides of their lineage. Since claim to lineage was vital to a Jew, there could hardly have been a bigger insult.

He likens Sarah to the "system" of religion that bears them, or the "city" that they live in. What he is saying is that in order to obtain inheritance, not only does one have to have the right father, but also you have to come from the right spiritual "womb." He tells the Judaizers that the womb, the system, the city, they were from collectively, determines whether or not you are an inheritor, not only one's father. Their "city" was not the womb of God. What he is doing is redefining Israel—the corporate entity, the people, the city of God.[19]

Paul likens the Jewish system to Sinai/Arabia and calls it bondage. Sinai/Arabia was the place they cursed themselves! We have seen in earlier chapters that it was the place where they promised Moses and the Lord that they would obey everything the law said to do.

Paul says nothing has changed since Moses' day. The Jerusalem brethren were still trying to put themselves and the Galatians under a curse that had proven historically to be faulty. The Jewish contingent was operating under the same religious pride and "we can do it spirit" of their forefathers. The law was inherently flawed, not because of the law itself, but because of the self-energized oath that Israel made. In the presence of God's holy commandments they said: "We can do it. Just tell us what to do. Not only can we do it, but we can do it without experiential contact with God. Please, do not talk to us relationally, just give us the requirements and we will keep them." Paul likens this slavery, bondage, self-condemning line of thought as being the "Jerusalem" from below. He says the Jerusalem from above is free. From her mother's womb come the covenant sons and heirs, not earthly Jerusalem.

PRECEPTS OR PERSONHOOD

Not much has changed. The performance-based legalist lives by principles and can only receive what he has earned—and lives boxed in himself and cannot know Father God's character.[20] The law was weak because of confidence in self-sufficiency. The modern legalist is kin to the Sinaitic Israelite.

Bible slingers, thumpers, and quoters by the thousands around the world are determined to obey God, yet know nothing of His life and Spirit. It is exactly these kind of people who will resist, rise up against, yes, and even murder the true sons of the covenant who live in life.[21] A man of principle will always be the first one to resist Spirit and life whenever it tries to manifest Christ in spiritual reality. The most principled people in the world resisted Jesus.

Gordon Dalbey summarizes it nicely: "The man who 'always does what is right' is the most dangerous threat to God's purposes in this world"[22] and "Jesus did not regard the 'pagan' as God's worst enemy, but rather men who used their religion to mask their brokenness...."[23] And finally, "For Jesus, Christian Enemy Number One is the religious man who claims to follow Jesus but in reality hides from him and Father God behind Law and 'principles.' "[24]

Now, one might say, how does Paul get away with all this? Well, to his critics, then and now, he doesn't! To his critics, all of Paul's thinking, and our Christian faith, is illegitimate. If Paul is wrong, we are all out of luck unless we are natural Jews!

WE HAVE A PROBLEM...

In Genesis 16, a problem has occurred *within* Abraham's household. Two sons are present: Ishmael, born of Abraham's own efforts, and Isaac, born of the promise of God. The presence of the two sons, or seeds, caused strife *within* Abraham's house. His family (and God's purpose through Abraham) was not threatened from outside forces, but rather from contention *within*.

Just as there was conflict *within* Abraham's house between the two seeds naturally, so it was in Galatia historically and in the Church today. There are always two seeds present within the Church that are sworn to eternal enmity. Paul realized the situation in Galatia required decisive corrective action.

God's attitude toward things that encroach upon His eternal purpose, His promise, and the preeminence of His Son, is decidedly politically incorrect and intolerant. When it comes to the preeminence of Christ in the Church, and the effects of subtle performance-based Christian legalism, there is no room for negotiation. If modern pastoral counselors had been present in Abraham's house (or in Galatia), they would have recommended Sarah, Hagar, and Abraham take courses in conflict resolution, stress management, family counseling, negotiating a "win-win" situation, sensitivity training, etc. That was not God's response.

After Paul presents the fact of the conflict between the two seeds, he contrasts the fruit of the two seeds: how Spirit-born and fleshly religionists behave *within* the house (see Gal. 5; 6). In other words, what do the two seeds look like when manifested in human behavior? Remember, Paul was speaking to *Christians* about manifesting the works of the flesh, *not* unredeemed sinners! The problem is in the house, not in the world!

Legalism and godless Christian religion are not harmless. Seeds bear fruit. The fruit of the slave seed of Ishmael is relational breakdown and a spirit of accusation loosed *within* the Church. The effective testimony of Christ can never peacefully cohabit with a spirit of accusation, which is the inevitable result of religion without Christ.

Only two of the works of the flesh listed in Galatians 5:19-21 are offenses against God: idolatry and witchcraft. The majority (16 out of 18) are breakdowns and breaches of interpersonal human relationships or sins manifested through what we speak. Paul exhorted the Galatians to be careful that they did not bite and devour one another (see Gal. 5:15). This is metaphorical language for nasty, vicious, mean-spirited, accusatorial, gossipy verbal comments designed to tear down and rend the Body of Christ. The fruit of legal Christian religion, biting and devouring one another, always:

- results from tolerating the legal seed of bondage in the Church.

- accuses others in their sin while excusing ourselves.

- masquerades as a concern for righteousness and the purpose of God.

Our "Christian" message has little credibility in the spirit realm or in the world. We cannot even get along ourselves. We claim to be the ministers of reconciliation—yet we cannot be reconciled. We try to export a message that we do not practice and it is thrown back in our faces by a disgusted world that is hungering for reality—Gospel reality. *No wonder they want to kill us.*

God's controversy is not primarily with the homosexuals, abortionists, and secular humanists. They are sinners and act like sinners. Why do we get so indignant about sinners acting the only way they know how? What do we expect? God's controversy is first with His own (see 1 Pet. 4:17). There is enough power in the true Seed to take care of those bound in sin. The true Gospel is the power of God unto salvation (see Rom. 1:16; 1 Cor. 1:18). It is often easier to bring a rank sinner to repentance than to turn a religionist from his or her Christ-less Christian religion.

How strategic our adversary is! How cunning to use Christ-less, performance-based, Christian religion to undermine what satan knows is the secret to his undoing: the manifestation of the true

Gospel in power. If the seed can be *corrupted* from *within*, then its *effectiveness without* is undermined. This issue is not a minor theological point. The essence of Gospel effectiveness is at stake and I hope you see it as clearly as I do.

CONCLUSION

Galatians is an ad hoc letter from a spiritual father to his children. Paul birthed the churches in Galatia through his missionary efforts and he writes with the passion of a father whose family is being threatened. Something was happening in Galatia that threatened his relationship with the churches and the essence of the Gospel. Paul was dealing with *real* people and *real life* issues—personalities, feelings, reputations, leadership issues, deep emotions, religious opinions, and religious traditions. Paul was not addressing theological abstractions. He was addressing life issues.

Paul's remedy for the seed of bondage and its fruit of accusation in the Church is the same as it was to Abraham in his house: *Cast out the slave woman and her seed!*[25] Galatians is not a dispassionate theological abstract, a position paper on a religious theory (in this case, justification by faith) tidily written to satisfy the intellectual and philosophical inquiry of Western scholars and theologians. If we treat it as such, we will invariably emphasize the intellectual, philosophical, and theological aspects of Paul's letter and miss its substance. Theology is the vehicle Paul uses to introduce us to a Person and another realm of life. We must not sanitize the passion and personality in this letter in the laundry of Western rationalism and comfortable middle-class ethics.

Paul's concern was not one of substituting one teaching for another, but rather how the Galatians were to live life. What does it mean to be a Christian? How or by what means is a Christian to live? Galatians is more than condemnation of an error in theology or a mistake in thinking—right thinking versus wrong thinking, right or wrong doctrine. Overcoming performance-based, legalistic religion is a battle for spiritual life. Wherever the reality of the experiential Spirit is minimized, de-emphasized, or avoided, a legalistic spirit will take its place. It matters not the name on the building, the orthodox creed, or spotless character. Without the manifested Spirit in gifts and fruit, legalism is the only alternative: Spirit-less Christian philosophy and teaching in the name of Christ.

Wherever performance, judgment, and measurement assume a role in the process of Christian maturity rather than life and liberty, a legalistic spirit has taken residence.

End Notes

1. I find it amazing and amusing that large segments of dispensational fundamentalism have no problem whatsoever in dismissing the applicability of entire sections of the Scriptures as irrelevant to the believer. E.W. Bullinger contended that the Gospels do not apply to believers in the present era and Lewis Sperry Chafer taught that only the Gospel of John, Acts, and the Epistles applied to the believer. Folks who think like these gentlemen would have a fit if someone should apply the same basic logic to a passage that they think should be universally applicable. It would seem the definition of who is faithful to the Scripture, or who is a "liberal" or not, depends on which portions someone chooses to ignore. Once the dispensational knife is out of the sheath, it cuts both ways.

2. It is routinely ignored by the masses of the well-meaning.

3. Galatians 5 and 6 deal primarily with ethical and responsible living, which should result from those who claim to be Spirit-sons. It is simply beyond the scope of this writing to examine those chapters in detail, other than to say, if we are fully inherited Spirit-sons, as I have been saying throughout this text, we should *act like it*. Galatians 5 and 6 are an integral part of the inheritance "package."

4. A literary device in which meaning is hidden or symbolized. In Paul's use of allegories he never discards

the historical facts. The distinctive feature of Christian interpretation is that if a passage has an allegorical interpretation, it does not violate or neutralize the literal or historical meaning. This distinguishes Paul from Gnostics and others who are always looking for "deeper" hidden meanings of the "deeper" truth in a passage beyond the literal meaning.

5. The astute reader might say, "What about Second Peter 1:5, which specifically tells us to add virtues?" Context, context, context. The admonition is preceded by: receipt of the promise, sharing in the divine nature, and having received everything we already need for life and godliness—all the points Paul makes in Galatians. The word translated "add" in the KJV is our friend we have seen earlier: *epichoregeo*. The point is, outfit yourself in these virtues because they have already been lavishly provided—get busy with it, *now* (aorist imperative active). Put on what has been given to you. Our outfitting in virtue is the result of being in Christ, not the means to being in Christ.

6. These five points are an extreme condensation from T.A. Sparks, *The Centrality and Supremacy of the Lord Jesus Christ* (Bethesda: Testimony Book Ministry, 1989). In general, I am deeply indebted to the entire corpus of T.A. Sparks writings for indelibly and eternally marking my soul with a passion for the centrality of the Person and work of Christ. I have read no other author who was so clear on what really matters, nor have I ever read another author who surpasses Sparks in his revelation and understanding of the cosmic significance of Christ and His cross. I am who I am today, in part, because of the writings of T.A. Sparks.

7. Don't smoke, don't drink, don't chew or run around with those who do!

8. A pretty good definition of spiritual maturity.

9. This gives a little zing to the account in Philemon, knowing that Philemon had the authority to have Onesimus executed under the Roman fugitive slave laws should he so desire. Paul was dealing with life and death issues. Many American Christians get offended if their leaders ask them to change pews—let alone advise them on a matter of forgoing one's legal rights.

10. In First Corinthians 13:11, Paul is referring to the Roman custom/ceremony of adoption, making an allusion to a point of spiritual maturity. The Corinthians needed to adjust their behavior to match their status in Christ as fully mature, adopted sons and daughters.

11. T.A. Sparks, *Centrality*, p. 43.

12. T.A. Sparks, *Centrality*, p. 43.

13. Paul declares in Galatians 6:17 that the physical marks in his body as the result of persecutions were the "stigmata" of his freedom. He understood, unlike ourselves, that freedom in Christ leaves a mark—a mark of a new master. We are free—free to serve God and others.

14. Gr. present imperative middle voice.

15. In the Greek, the crying is associated with the word *spirit*, so that it is the Spirit who is doing the crying.

16. Gr. *kradzo*: a loud and earnest cry or public announcement.

17. Galatians 5:12 literally says, "I would that they would emasculate (mutilate) themselves. If cutting off a little foreskin makes one a covenant son, then cutting off the whole thing might do it more thoroughly! Have at it!" This is Paul's language.

18. I am indebted to Dr. Ron Cottle, President of Christian Life School of Theology, for this information that I gleaned while a student in his class/course on Galatians.

19. The city is a metaphor for the people. In our culture when we say "Washington" or "New York," they can be metaphors for the people of the city. The city represents the people collectively.

20. Gordon Dalbey, *Sons of the Father* (Wheaton: Tyndale House, 1992), p. 200.

21. Jesus said if we hate in our heart we are guilty of murder. We do not use stone anymore; we use gossip and accusation.

22. Dalbey, *Sons of the Father*, p. 191.

23. Dalbey, *Sons of the Father*, p. 195.

24. Dalbey, *Sons of the Father*, p. 195-196.

25. This is not referring to literal people, but dealing severely with the spirit of performance-based religion that would encroach upon the Person and work of Christ.

Parting Shots and Thoughts

I have tried to present performance-based religion as the nefarious spirit that it is. I have equally attempted to show God's abundant remedy in the New Covenant and the indwelling Spirit of sonship. I would like to close with a short diagnostic checklist addressing these two major points: Why is legalism so effective and what can I do about it practically?

WHY IS LEGALISM SO EFFECTIVE AND APPEALING?

- It is easy. Even a dog can be conditioned to obey.

- It is clearly defined. There is no need for discernment in areas where the Scriptures are silent.

- I can understand the Bible with my intellect. To know the Spirit as a Person is just "too weird."

- It is easy to lead and control people with it. Guilt and condemnation are the handmaidens of the religious demagogue.

- It promotes a false security. If everything is clearly defined, at least you can tell how well you are doing against the list.

- I don't have to work through relational difficulties. I can just separate from the brother or sister who is just "not living up to the standard"; after all, I don't want my kids contaminated.

- It appears righteous. Ain't no fleas on me.

- It provides psychological feelings of superiority. Hey, at least I am holier than my neighbor.

- It is easier to perform to code than to die and be resurrected. Slavery looks better than death.

- Others will accept me if I meet their expectations.

- Life is formal, neatly pressed and packaged, orderly. No troubled waters cross the bow of the religionist's ship. Life is neatly managed by principle.

- Keeping a few rules is less costly than being a living sacrifice.

How Can I Break Free of Performance-Based Religion's Gravitational Pull?

- By revelation. It starts by recognizing personal need and God's abundant resource.

- Receive Christ's forgiveness and the Spirit's indwelling as an *experiential reality*. I don't care how you get it, when you get it, or what you do when you get it…but get it you must!

- Fellowship among a free people. Legalism tends to rub off—so does liberty.

- Commune with God by His Word and Spirit. Make it a life priority. Christianity simply does not work without it. Christian religion does, but not Christianity.

- Be honest with yourself. Tell it like it is: to yourself, your peers, your pastor, and your God.

- Avoid wooden, simplistic, naïve interpretations of difficult passages of Scripture. Do some digging on your own. Read opinions other than your group's or denomination's view. Look for consensus across as broad a spectrum of theological opinions as you can find. If you can't find consensus, pray like crazy and don't project your opinions on others.

- Maintain a Christ-centered consciousness, not sin consciousness.

- Face any difficulty, discomfort, or uneasiness necessary to maintain relational unity.

- Don't make minor doctrinal conformity the basis of major Christian unity.

- Don't sweat the small stuff.

- Keep the *main thing* (Christ and Him crucified) the *main thing*.

- Exercise diligent guard against falling back. If it can happen in Galatia, it can happen anywhere, to anybody.

- Submit to leaders who are free. It takes leaders who themselves are free to free a people.

- Focus on the Great Commandment. The Holy Spirit is well able to work out character issues in those whose river is flowing in love and service to others. He will *personally see to it* that you are misunderstood, hated, despised, rejected, ripped-off, betrayed, let down, hurt, taken advantage of, accused, cheated on, slandered, abused, misused, and lied about by the people you are trying to love and serve. He is *really good* at this stuff. There will be plenty of opportunity for character development! Character development doesn't happen in the lab atmosphere of church services. It happens in the arena of life.

- Emphasize love and service in teaching and preaching, not character transformation, duty, and responsibility.

- Avoid comparison like the plague.

- Don't project your convictions on other people.

Finally, I would like to let a few voices from a diverse theological spectrum close this book with their complimentary thoughts on these vital matters. Sometimes the only prophets God's people pay attention to are the dead ones.

Here is what A.W. Tozer had to say:

What is generally overlooked is that Fundamentalism, as it spread throughout the various denominations and non-denominational groups, fell victim to its own virtues. The Word died in the hands of its friends. Verbal inspiration, for instance (a doctrine which I have always held), soon became afflicted with rigor mortis. The voice of the prophet was silenced and the scribe captured the minds of the faithful. In large areas the religious imagination withered. An unofficial hierarchy decided what Christians were to believe. Not the Scriptures, but what the scribe thought the Scriptures meant became the Christian creed. Christian colleges, seminaries, Bible institutes, Bible conferences, popular Bible expositors all joined to promote the cult of textualism. The system of extreme dispensationalism which was devised, relieved the Christian of repentance, obedience and cross-carrying in any other than the most formal sense. Whole sections of the New Testament were taken from the Church and disposed of after a rigid system of "dividing the word of truth."

All this resulted in a religious mentality inimical to the true faith of Christ. A kind of cold mist settled over Fundamentalism...the basic doctrines were there, but the climate was just not favorable to the sweet fruits of the Spirit...the doctrines were sound but something vital was missing. The tree of correct doctrine was never allowed to blossom. The voice of the turtle [dove] was rarely heard in the land; instead, the parrot sat on his artificial perch and dutifully repeated what he had been taught and the whole emotional tone was somber and dull.... As the letter triumphed, the Spirit withdrew and textualism ruled supreme. It was the time of the believer's Babylonian captivity.... The error of textualism is not doctrinal. It is far more subtle than that and much more difficult to discover, but its effects are just as deadly. Not its theological beliefs are at fault, but its assumptions.

It assumes for instance, that if we have the word for a thing we have the thing itself. If it is in the Bible, it is in us. If we have the doctrine, we have the experience. If something was true of Paul it is of necessity true of us because we accept Paul's epistles as divinely inspired. The Bible tells us how to be saved, but textualism goes on to make it something which in the very nature of things it cannot do. Assurance of individual salvation is thus no more than a logical conclusion drawn from doctrinal premises, and the resultant experience wholly mental.

Then came the revolt. The human mind can endure textualism just so long before it seeks a way of escape. So, quietly and quite unaware that any revolt was taking place, the masses of Fundamentalism reacted, not from the teaching of the Bible but from the mental tyranny of the scribes.[1]

T.A. Sparks wrote:

Touch religious traditions and established orders and you will find the same thing Stephen met, a jealousy which issues from blindness to the vastly greater purpose of God.

It is impressive how any stand for a true expression of the Body of Christ is fraught with more conflict than anything else…let there be a movement in the direction of real corporate expression of a Holy Spirit constituted testimony to Christ corporate, then the battle is on and nothing will be untried to break that up, discredit it, or in some way nullify that testimony…A true representation of the elect Body of Christ is a standing menace and ominous sign to the Satanic kingdom because it is the Church which—at last—is going to dispossess and supplant the 'world-rulers' of this darkness and govern with Christ.[2]

William Law says:

There is no degree of delusion higher than that which is evidenced by those who profess to teach from the divinely inspired Scriptures that the immediate, continual illumination and working of the Spirit in men's hearts ceased when the canon of Scripture was complete. To deny the present prophetic gift in the church is to deny also that very manifestation of Christ today to His own which the Scriptures teach is the only means to the reality of Gospel Christianity.[3]

A.B. Simpson wrote:

This [the indwelling Holy Spirit to continue Jesus' life and ministry and to perpetuate miracles] is the mighty gift of our ascended Lord. This is the supreme need of the church today.[4]

Andrew Murray wrote:

The indwelling must be accepted and treasured until it becomes part of the consciousness of the new man: the Holy Spirit possesses me.[5]

EPILOGUE

End Notes

1. Taken from *Keys to the Deeper Life* by A. W. Tozer. Copyright © 1957 by Sunday Magazine 1987 by Zondervan Publishing Corporation.

2. Sparks, T. A. *The Stewardship of the Mystery.* Bethesda, MD: Testimony book Ministry, 1989. Public domain.

3. From *The Power of the Spirit* by William Law. Copyright © 1971, CLC Publications, Fort Washington, PA. Used by Permission.

4. Reprinted from *The Holy Spirit* by A. B. Simpson, © N.D. by Christian Publications, Inc. Used by permission of Christian Publications, Inc., 800.233.4443, www.christianpublications.com.

5. From *The Spirit of Christ* by Andrew Murray. Copyright © 1977, Marshall, Morgan & Scott. Published by CLC Publications. Used by Permission.

Works Cited

Alley, John Kingsley. *The Apostolic Revelation.* Rockhampton: Peace Publishing, 2002.

Bauer, Walter. *A Greek-English Lexicon of the New Testament and Other Early Christian Literature.* Edited by W.F. Arndt and F.W. Gingrich. 2nd. ed. revised by F.W. Gingrich and F.W. Danker. Chicago, IL: University of Chicago Press, 1979.

Blanchard, John. *Gathered Gold.* Hertfordshire, UK: Evangelical Press, 1984.

Bosworth, Fred F. *Christ the Healer.* Old Tappan, NJ: Fleming H. Revell, 1973.

Bynum, Juanita. Unknown source.

Chambers, Oswald. *My Utmost for His Highest.* Westwood: Barbour and Co., Inc., 1963.

Cottle, Ronald E. *Galatians.* Columbus: Christian Life Publishers, 1997.

Dalbey, Gordon. *Sons of the Father.* Wheaton: Tyndale House, 1992.

Eldredge, John. *Wild at Heart: Discovering the Secret of a Man's Soul.* Nashville: Thomas Nelson, 2001.

Epstein, Barbara L. *Politics of Domesticity: Women, Evangelism and Temperance in Nineteenth Century America.* Middletown, Conn.: Wesleyan University Press, 1981.

Friberg, Timothy, B. Friberg, and Neva Miller. *Analytical Lexicon of the Greek New Testament.* Grand Rapids: Baker, 2000.

Fee, Gordon. *God's Empowering Presence.* Peabody: Hendrickson, 1994.

Gill, John. *Exposition of the Entire Bible.* Downloaded from e-Sword at: http://www.e-sword.net, Rick Meyers, 2002.

Hölé, J. Konrad. *You Were Born a Champion, Don't Die a Loser.* Minneapolis: World Press, 1999.

Keener, Craig S., ed. *IVP Background Commentary: New Testament.* Downers Grove: Intervarsity Press. Retrieved from: Quick Verse 7.0, CD-ROM. Cedar Rapids: Parsons Technology, 1993. Electronic Edition STEP Files, 1997.

Klystra, Chester, and Betsy Kylstra. *Restoring the Foundations: Counseling by the Living Word.* Santa Rosa: Proclaiming His Word, 1994.

Law, William. *The Power of the Spirit.* Fort Washington: Christian Literature Crusade, 1993.

Lloyd-Jones, D. Martin. *The Sovereign Spirit.* Wheaton: Harold Shaw Publishers, 1985.

Malina, Bruce. J., and Richard L. Rohrbaugh. *Social Science Commentary on the Synoptic Gospels.* Minneapolis: Fortress, 1992.

_____. *Social Science Commentary on the Gospel of John.* Minneapolis: Fortress, 1998.

McManus, Erwin R. *An Unstoppable Force: Daring to Be the Church God Has in Mind.* Loveland: Group Publishing, 2001.

McReynolds, Paul R. *Word Study Greek-English New Testament.* Wheaton: Tyndale, 1990.

Moody, Dwight L. *Secret Power.* Ventura: Regal Books, 1987.

Murray, Andrew. *The Spirit of Christ.* Fort Washington: Christian Literature Crusade, nd.

Works Cited

Podles, Leon J. *The Church Impotent: The Feminization of Christianity.* Dallas: Spence Publishing Co. 1999.

Peck, M. Scott. *The People of the Lie.* New York: Touchstone, 1983.

Simpson, A.B. *The Holy Spirit.* Vol. I and II. Harrisburg: Christian Publishing, n.d.

Sparks, T. Austin. *The Stewardship of the Mystery.* Vol. I and II. Bethesda: Testimony Book Ministry, 1989.

_____. *The Centrality and Universality of the Cross.* Bethesda: Testimony Book Ministry, reprint, 1988.

_____. *The Centrality and Supremacy of the Lord Jesus Christ.* Bethesda: Testimony Book Ministry, reprint, 1989.

Strachan, Gordon. *The Pentecostal Theology of Edward Irving.* Peabody: Hendrickson, 1988.

Thayer, J.H. *The New Thayer's Greek-English Lexicon.* J.P. Green, Sr., ed. Peabody: Hendrickson, 1981.

Tozer, A.W. *God Tells the Man Who Cares.* Harrisburg: Christian Publications, 1970.

_____. *Keys to the Deeper Life.* Grand Rapids: Zondervan, 1973.

Vine, W.E. *Vine's Complete Expository Dictionary of Old and New Testament Words.* M.F. Unger and W. White, Jr., eds. Nashville: Thomas Nelson, 1996.

Zodhiates, Spiros. *The Complete Word Study New Testament.* Chattanooga: AMG Publishers, 1991.

_____. *The Hebrew-Greek Key Study Bible.* Chattanooga: AMG Publishers, 1988.